This book is for you if...

You are a Head Teacher
- Who wants results that will impact both staff and students
- Who wants all students to access the curriculum to the best of their ability
- Who has a number of staff dealing with a challenging student on a regular basis
- Who would like to give young people confidence with exams, challenges and change
- Who has identified vulnerable young people who would benefit from empowerment
- With a budget looking for a service that is achieving 92% positive change in just six sessions
- Who wants fast, effective and measurable results

You are a Teacher / SENCO
- Who is worried about the emotional health and well-being of your students
- That would like school transfers to be a positive experience
- Who would like all students to participate and be productive in lessons
- Who has identified students with low confidence and low self-esteem
- Who is aware of challenges outside of school and want to help
- Who finds teaching stressful
- Who would like to teach

You are a Parent
- Who is worried about your child
- Who has noticed that your child is unhappy and withdrawn
- Who does not know what to do with your child's behaviour
- Would like your child to have confidence and self-esteem
- Whose child is being bullied, self-harming or not coping with life
- Who would like to get on better with your child or as a family
- Who wants to see your child happy

You are a Young Person
- Who has a problem and does not know where to turn
- Who cannot see how to move forward
- Who would like to fit in
- Who would like to get on at home or at school
- Who may not want to partake in talking therapies
- Who wants to know how to make the changes that you want in your life
- Who would like to be happy

What people are saying about Jepeca

"Jepeca makes a genuine difference to the young children they work with. Where traditional counselling has been unsuccessful, Jepeca's programme has empowered young people to take control of their lives and shape their own futures. The Jepeca programme has been particularly successful with children who are extremely vulnerable. Young people respond well to their forward-looking, optimistic approach."

Jacquie Martin – BSc Psych Hon, Cambridge Cert SEN Management
Secondary School (2014)

"I cannot comment on individual children's experiences of the coaching. I am in a position to feedback that we as an organisation, concerned with supporting children, are very happy with the reported outcomes. We have found the programme to be accessible to a wide range of children in our schools. It is focused and not a time-consuming programme, which is attractive to schools as children are not missing large chunks of learning. Schools have reported to me that they like the programme and are keen for students to access the programme. The feedback from the individual children that have received the coaching is overwhelmingly positive. It is great that Jepeca have designed a form that makes it easy to measure impact. I cannot recommend them highly enough."

Sally Gubb
ASPECTS Partnership development manager (2013)

"I am only too pleased to help spread to other schools and young people the excellent service which you provide."

Deputy Head
Secondary School

"From our first meeting I was totally impressed with Julianne's professionalism, enthusiasm and sheer commitment to her Empowerment Coaching programme. The impact of Julianne's work with students was swift and significant with parents calling to say what a positive difference Julianne had made to their child's emotional well-being. From a student's perspective, Julianne's involvement resulted in a student feeling 'magical' after only six weeks' work. From a school's perspective, Julianne's work was rated as the singular most effective intervention that the school had seen in several years. Highly recommended."

Joy Cox
Extended Schools (2011)

"One of my children has been suffering for the last few years with extreme emotional difficulties and bullying, which has been the result of some very traumatic times...I am thrilled to say that I have found the most wonderful lady...Julianne Hadden who runs a company called Jepeca Empowerment Coaching...This coaching, after just two sessions, has made a dramatic difference to his life, and I truly recommend that, if you know of any child that can benefit from this service, you speak to your school or get in touch with her directly. This is a truly amazing service and Julianne has made a real difference to many young people's lives."

Parent

"The Jepeca programme has made such a positive difference to both teachers and students. Thank you."

Teacher

"Jepeca has taught me how to control my anger.
It has helped a lot with family stuff
and my behaviour at school.

People say I am behaving better than I used to.
I don't argue with my dad and when he
asks me to do something, I just do it.
I feel happier.
Recently I haven't been hitting my brother or sister.

The Jepeca programme will change your life;
it is exciting and has fun activities."

About the Author

Julianne Hadden founded Jepeca in 2009. Her background is in the National Health Service, where she was a qualified nurse and midwife, and in education, where she practiced as a school nurse, giving her first-hand experience in dealing with many professions including CAMHS, the police, schools, social services and child protection.

Having visibility of the processes supporting child protection was a turning point for Julianne. This experience allowed her to see how very little emotional support was given to vulnerable young people when faced with challenging situations, environments or difficult circumstances. She decided then that she wanted to be part of the solution, and so Jepeca was born!

The Jepeca programme empowers people by enhancing their essential life skills and natural abilities so they can confidently deal with life's challenges and changes, resulting in happy, in control and productive individuals and members of society.

"I think more positively about myself
and am more confident in class.
I can put my hand up and volunteer now;
before, I couldn't.

My mum has noticed and my school
has told her I am more confident.
I don't know why but I just feel better.
I am much calmer,
confident and happier.

This was fun."

The Jepeca Way

A simple intervention to empower
young people to get back in control
of their lives and make lasting,
positive change

Jepeca
Inspiring Happiness

by Julianne Hadden

Published by
Filament Publishing Ltd
16, Croydon Road, Waddon, Croydon,
Surrey, CR0 4PA, United Kingdom
Telephone +44 (0)20 8688 2598
Fax +44 (0)20 7183 7186
info@filamentpublishing.com
www.filamentpublishing.com

ISBN - 978-1-910125-18-2

Printed by CreateSpace

Dedicated to my husband, Kenny Hadden.
You are the wind beneath my wings.

Acknowledgements

Starting at the very beginning, I want to thank my parents, Margaret and Humphrey Counihan, for my fun, happy and memorable childhood. Together with my brothers and sister and many aunts, uncles and, of course, cousins, I have enough memories to last me well into old age.

I'd like to thank my gorgeous husband, Kenny Hadden; without you, none of this would be possible! Thank you to Jessica, Peter and Caitlin Hadden, who make life worth living.

Thanks also goes to Tracey Ferguson, who is available 24/7, Aine O'Brien for the headspace, and to Mags and Ciaran Earls for filling in, as and when! Thanks to Michelle Banks for listening, Muireann Coyle for the tea, Diane and Mark Vidler for the company, and to Sarah and Rick Hassett, and Mary and Stan D'Souza for the loan of their children. Hair by Jackie! Thanks to Carmel Doherty for making me look good, and to Jennifer Carpenter for making the rest of ye look good!

Thank you, Nicola Merton Richards, for ringing the bell and waking me up!

Thank you, Joy Cox, for believing in me and the Jepeca programme in January 2011.

Thank you to all our Jepeca coaches who are changing lives and making my dream a reality every day – especially my right-hand woman, Katie Dommett. Everyone should have a Katie!

Thank you to Chris Day and his team at Filament for bringing 'The Jepeca Way' to the world.

Thanks to my friends who support and remember to remove me from work now and again!

For those that are not on this plane, I know you are routing for me :) Keep it up!

Finally, I want to thank all those who have accessed the programme. You are my inspiration and I applaud your refusal to accept the unacceptable.

Contents

"The Jepeca programme was fun and has helped
my whole family with anger.

I wasn't very confident and didn't like going out.
I feel more confident now and
speak my mind more -
in a good way.

I also participate in conversations now.
I found who I am."

The Problem

Before I start, please understand that everybody (well, the majority of people) are doing the best they can with what they have at the minute. We cannot change anyone else, we can only change ourselves, but when we change ourselves, everyone and everything around us changes too!

I feel it is important to stress this, as in my experience everyone who comes in to contact with young people, from teachers, head teachers, dinner ladies, cleaners, caretakers, bus drivers, social workers, doctors, nurses, police therapists and hospital workers, are doing their best (if it were money that were driving them, they would be working in the city, I should think). Unfortunately, there are many times when their best is not enough!

For example, I have just had a call from a very worried and concerned mother whose daughter is anorexic and is not yet receiving any kind of help that she feels is making a difference, and this is eight months later. There are many services involved but neither the mother or daughter feel they are working. After the call, I received the following text message: "Thank you. I wish I had called you sooner. I feel like I am actually making steps to help my daughter now". I just explained the programme and what we would do over six sessions.

Jepeca needs to be available to every young person. This young person is lucky to have a mother that will stop at nothing to find her the help that she thinks will make a difference. The services that are involved currently are doing their best, but it is not good enough for this girl, not good enough for her mother, and unfortunately they are not alone. We are getting more and more calls from desperate parents who are unhappy with the services being offered.

Times are changing but the services available to concerned parents do not seem to be taking on board their comments, thoughts and concerns. Young people that have accessed other services before they get to the Jepeca programme are generally expecting an experience similar to what they have had before. Thankfully, that is not the case! We are used to hearing how different we are and, judging by the huge smile our clients have going out the door after their sessions, I for one am very pleased.

The problem with this is that most people talk about it as if it were the norm, acceptable, so to speak, whilst in actual fact the problem is what has got you where you are and that is where you shall remain until you find a solution. So, who is looking for the solution? Usually the parents. The majority of schools want things to improve but I have experienced school that said they were just ticking a box, whether the solution was right for the young person or not. When I first started Jepeca, I thought about what young people who are facing challenges and changes would need (a solution) and created the programme they're after, not the other way round!

This chapter will contain statistics and costs, but do not let this turn you off reading it. I know that statistics and costs can sound like a difficult tiresome read, but, nonetheless, it is vital to understand why the Jepeca solution is necessary and essential for all young people. In fact, I think I can safely say that you will be surprised with the numbers of young people who face challenges and difficult circumstances on a regular basis, and that you at some point will encounter these young people during your lifetime. Failing that, just think that the next generation will probably be responsible for your health and well-being at some point and now is your chance to ensure that you have done your best for them!

Interestingly, there was a 'World Happiness Report 2013' which was edited by John Helliwell, Richard Layard and Jeffrey Sachs. Lord Richard Layard, of the London School of Economics, and the UK Government's 'happiness tsar' hailed the publication of the report, and went on to say that poor mental health – which can reduce life expectancy at the same rate as smoking – is highlighted as one of the biggest issues affecting the nation's happiness. **And 'emotional health' in childhood is singled out as the most important factor effecting adult well-being.** Lord Layard stated: "It has a major influence on children's subsequent success – their relationships, physical health and whether they can get a good job. Help is needed now to raise young people's level of emotional health and well-being and the answer does not always lie in training or counselling, often the default solutions put forward to address the problem in today's modern institutions." I agree, what a wise man. Yet how many people have heard or know about that report?

The Office for National Statistics also produced a report in 2012 measuring national well-being of children aged 0-15 years. It mentions that it is now largely accepted that what children become in their adult life is to a great extent a product of their experiences in the early stages of their lives (Aldgate et al, 2010). According to the 2011 census, there were just over 10.5 million children aged 0 to 15 in England and Wales, which is about one in five of the population compared with one in three in 1911, which was attributed to the reduction in family size and improvement in medicine, health services and care of the elderly.

Here are some interesting facts mentioned in the survey. Smoking, drinking and drug use among young people in England (SDDS) found that 45% of 11 to 15-year-old pupils had drunk alcohol at least once. That is incredible. Let's say you take an average class of 30 young people; that is nearly half that have drunk alcohol!

Research has shown that among children starting primary school, those that have had pre-school education tend to be more confident, more sociable and have more developed cognitive function than those who have not had pre-school education exposure. Children from disadvantaged backgrounds have also been found to have benefited significantly from good quality childcare and early learning as it allows mixing children from different social backgrounds (Sylva, 2004). Interesting!

A study analysing the Millennium Cohort Study of siblings of children born around 2000 (Goodman and Gregg, 2010) found that several other factors affected a child's cognitive development, such as:

- Children who go to nursery and private school tend to have higher cognitive test scores than those who do not.

- Children whose parents think they are very or fairly likely to go to university tend to have higher test scores than those whose parents are pessimistic.

- Children who read for enjoyment also tend to have higher cognitive test scores than those who do not.

I reckon at least two out of three of the above is achievable for most people. The problem is you have to rely on other people and, as we know, you cannot change anyone else, you can only change yourself. You would need parents to be supportive and that is just not possible for every parent.

Data from Understanding Society showed that in the UK, 96% of children aged 10 to 15 years had computer access at home. Computer use for educational purposes in the home was also found to be high, with just over 80% of children using a computer at least once a month for homework or coursework. The same survey, collected between 2009 and 2010, showed that a higher proportion of boys (96%) than girls (89%) had at least one games console in their home. Girls, on the other hand, are more likely (90%) to have their own mobile phone than boys (84%).

In my experience, the clients we have worked with spend a considerable amount of time in their rooms on their own screen watching, be it mobile phones or gaming. Girls do tend to think their life is their phone, and their phone is their life. This can and has been the result of class exclusions and school exclusions when confiscated. The link between behaviour and gaming, regardless of age appropriate games, is well researched, yet many young people continue to spend hour after hour totally immersed in a reality that does not exist.

The National Statistics report says, for children, there is a connection between the length of time for which they use media and their well-being. Research in 2011 from the Institute for Social and Economic Research (ISER) reported that children in the UK who had access to games consoles, computer games and internet use at home for less than an hour on a normal school day also reported better well-being than those who used these facilities for four hours or more. Children who spend too much time chatting online may also be at risk of unwanted attention and harassment (Skew et al, 2011)

Cyberbullying is one form of unwanted attention and harassment that affects many young people today. It is unthinkable that one person's misfortune or misery is entrainment for others, yet it appears to be the case. The Virtual Violence II, released by charity BeatBullying, said 350,222 children were experiencing cyberbullying, with nearly a quarter facing the problem for a year or more. An article on www.publicservice.co.uk mentions how 20% of children and young people experiencing cyberbullying were said to have indicated a reluctance to go to school due to their fear of cyberbullies, with 14% said to be living in fear. Living in FEAR! In this day and age, many are living in fear for reasons beyond their control, yet living in fear from cyberbullying in a developed country with educated people just doesn't make sense.

"I love the Jepeca programme and I love you.
It has helped me with everything.
I have noticed that I am a very charming boy
since you came to help me
and even my dog has noticed a difference.

Since you came into my life, you have helped me with a lot.
I am not annoying people
and I feel like I have changed my personality.
I feel more confident, happy
and can control my feelings calmly."

The Jepeca Programme – where it all began...

Hello, and welcome to the world of Jepeca.

We are a coaching company that really makes a difference.

We do not just say we make a difference; we know we make a difference, and we have the paperwork to prove it. Our journey had seen us work with many different young people (which we call clients) from different walks of life, who are all looking for an answer to their problem, or problems.

The Jepeca programme is fast, effective and measurable. Yes, that is right; as I said earlier, we do have the paperwork to prove it! Fast, as in every programme is run over six consecutive weeks. When you think about it, that is only six hours! Yet the transformations are amazing. Again, we have the paperwork! Effective, as in we have a 92% positive change record with every client referred to Jepeca. And measurable, as in we calibrate every single client in week one and again in week six.

The transition is evident to the client and the coach as well as anyone who knows the client. From here we give a report of the process through the six weeks. We also like to get feedback from whoever is involved in the day-to-day routine of the client so they can appreciate the difference and share their observations.

I suppose in order for you to fully understand the Jepeca programme, I should take you back in time where the dream became a reality. Only in my case, it was - the nightmare became a reality and I discovered that I was part of the problem. You don't need to bring anything with you; just your imagination and an open mind, and perhaps some tissues!

My name is Julianne Hadden and I am the founder of the Jepeca programme. I have much experience of people, situations, circumstances and life that I put down to luck, timing and, I have to say, destiny. The name of the company is Jepeca and it has a very personal meaning as it was cleverly created by my husband and contains part of the names of our three children

– Jessica, Peter and Caitlin. The coincidences along the way have been incredible and welcomed, the journey interesting and memorable, and the company appreciated and priceless.

It all began a few years ago. I was working as a school health nurse (basically, that means that I was part of a primary care trust working with several schools, professionals and young people). As part of my job role, I was involved in child protection, health education, government initiatives and immunisation programmes. We frequently held drop-in clinics in our secondary or high schools to provide a point of contact for young people who wanted to discuss issues in private, although this was also one of the first services to be dropped when the workload was in excess of the staffing levels!

School health is an essential department within a primary care trust; full of vibrant characters and hard-working people, especially nurses. Many of the school health staff went above and beyond the call of duty regularly, spending many hours attending to issues, problems and situations that make a real difference to the young people and parents. This is where I learned the importance of a manager and I will be forever thankful for their understanding and patience. I have many fond memories of my time in school health, but as with many departments in government-run organisations, my frustration grew as our voice shrunk! For me, the only way was out... and this is how it unfolded...

On this particular occasion, it was approaching summer and I was working in a school with a lovely young man. He had brought his friend with him for support. It was not the first time I had seen this young man (whom I shall call Colin to protect his identity). On his previous visits, Colin would make very little eye contact and always had his head down looking at the ground or his sore, bitten fingers. He whispered a lot and was always saying sorry and how stupid he was and he couldn't do anything right. He had always come to see me on his own, stayed for as long as he could and dragged his heels when it was time to return to class. I remember he always made sure to have an appointment to see me on my next visit.

During our last consultation, Colin arrived with his friend so I had a feeling that something was going to be disclosed if and when he felt the time was right. After a little while, he revealed that his father was physically abusing him at home. He would shout at him and hit him regularly. Colin couldn't understand why he was so horrible, but he was glad that his little brother escaped unharmed!

It had taken a serious amount of courage for him to speak out. He was, as you can imagine, visibly upset, shaking, crying and his voice trembled as he recalled the vile things his dad had said. He begged me to help him, as he was scared to go home. But he was also scared not to go home as his younger brother would be left alone with his dad and he said he needed to protect him. I assured him I would do what I could! And there in lies the initial problem.

I contacted the various individuals necessary to make a decision about Colin and his immediate future. After handing over to the appropriate adult within the school, I learned that this was not the first time that Colin had made allegations. Nor was it the first time that something was apparently done about it!!!

Confused?

So was I.

When I left Colin and his friend, he was relieved that something was going to be done and his friend was comforting him. Awaiting the bright, peaceful and exciting future that awaits all young people – right?

If it's a fairy-tale ending you are hoping for, do not read further... you have been warned!

Wrong. A bright, peaceful and exciting future does not await all young people. There, I said it. Were you shocked? I was. I thought I was making a difference! The reality was that I was part of the problem.

The problem being a system that allows young people to remain in situations, environments and circumstances with no emotional skills to deal with them. The repercussions are evident throughout the country in each county, community and school today. But that is for another chapter!

Back to Colin. As the summer holidays approached, Colin's family had a visit from social services and he remained within his family home with his father and younger brother, as before. Nothing had changed.

Nothing had changed for Colin, and for that, I am extremely sorry.

For me, the whole world had changed. I handed in my notice. I had let Colin down and I no longer wanted to be part of a system that allows young people who ask for help to be abandoned or left with empty promises.

I remember telling my wonderful, patient husband my plan. He said, "Julianne, you can't change the world," and I got really annoyed. I just turned to him and said, "I can and I will. I will just start with one person at a time."

My plan was to become part of the solution for every child and therein begins the next chapter.... The Jepeca programme was born and my naive excitement saw me through the negativity that accompanies such great adventures!

The Jepeca Programme – in a nutshell

After many months of writing, gathering and consolidating information, which comes from many years of experience, (not that I am very old!) I developed the following programme.

As mentioned previously, it is fast, effective and measurable, and one of the commonest words we hear from our clients is that they feel happier; either happier in their heart, happier in their head or they don't know why but they just they got happier. So mission accomplished.

The information gatherings I refer to are the needs of the young people who are in vulnerable or challenging situations, environments or circumstances. Once I had thought through the various ways that a young person could be hurt, upset, destructive or disempowered, I knew what they needed to be empowered, happy, productive and in control. Easy.

The information consolidating refers to putting the programme together. My experience in child protection conferences and child protection training courses, school health nursing and education, RGN (registered general nursing), midwifery, anger management, stress and time management, hypnotherapy, life coaching, NLP practitioner, NLP master and NLP trainer, BACP certificates in counselling skills level 2 and counselling studies level 3, as well as raising my own three amazing children, allowed me to put together a solid structured yet flexible programme to provide a solution that not only works but provides results time and time again.

My vision is to empower people, especially young people, to understand, utilise and develop their confidence, self-esteem, and emotional health and well-being to the best of their ability, so that they can live happy, productive and empowered lives. What more could anyone want?

The Jepeca programme provides tools, technique and strategies which people can refer to time and time again, with reliable and lasting effect. We as Jepeca coaches show you the way, but you are the only one who can make the changes you want to see in your life. You will see, as you read on, the programme is very simple. And simple is what we want; well, it was good enough for Einstein! *"Make everything as simple as possible, but not simpler,"* said Albert Einstein.

Or perhaps Caprice Bourret had the right idea, *"Things are simple, it is us human beings that make it difficult."* Totally agree! Amelia Barr said, *"It is always the simple that produces the marvelous."* Again, wise words but be careful how you read it! *"Never underestimate the power of a simple tool,"* said Craig Bruce. *"The solutions are all simple – after you have arrived at them. But they're simple only when you know already what they are,"* said Robert M. Pirsig. So if simple is good enough for them, it is good enough for me :)

We have a solution that provides individual solutions for both adults and young people. This book is dedicated to young people and inspiring their happiness, but I feel it is important to mention the Jepeca programme and adults. A brief word about using the programme with adults; the process is the same, just tailored to adults. The results are the same, just measured by the individual. The adults are the same, just happier.

The interesting thing when working with adults is that they always assume to know what the problem is, yet they persist in having the problem! Surely if you know what the problem is, you would know what to do about it? Or how to not have the problem? Yet there are many adults that spend years and years with the same problems! The mind boggles...

For example, one lady I worked with had been in a job which she hated. Over the years, what began as a niggling thought had grown to such an enormous significant yet imposing reality that she was unable to sleep and had physical symptoms, which led to relationship difficulties. Sounds crazy, doesn't it? She already had the answers. She already knew what she had to do. The process of the Jepeca programme empowered her to understand, develop and then utilise to the best of her ability the answers she knew that would make the changes that she needed.

Understanding, recognising and utilising your thoughts, feelings, emotions, filters and communication empowers everyone to achieve and succeed – in a way that is right for them.

The Jepeca Pilot

After providing a detailed presentation to a forward-thinking ESCO (Extended School Co-ordinator), head teachers, and SENCOs (Special Educational Needs Co-ordinators) attached to a consortium of schools in Hertfordshire in the UK at the end of 2010, my dream became a reality. Two weeks after the pilot started, I was signed up for the rest of that year. The results were evident after two weeks and the support from teachers, parents, and the commissioner confirmed what I already knew – the Jepeca programme changes lives. It is fast, effective and measurable and, most importantly, it inspires happiness and empowers each of its clients.

The following contains information about the initial pilot, results, feedback and an update a year later. Jepeca has since grown, but we are still in contact with, and commissioned to work within, the schools that partook in the original pilot of 2011. Our reputation precedes us, as the majority of our work is from word of mouth and referrals by clients, parents, teachers, head teachers, SENCOs and/or other professionals who are aware of the impact the Jepeca programme has.

The Jepeca programme has empowered many young people in the last three years and we have many enquiries from individuals and professionals as to how it came about. The following will answer some of those questions.

Pilot

In January 2011, a pilot was commissioned by an Extended School Co-ordinator (ESCO) in a consortium of schools within Hertfordshire, UK to assess the benefits of the Jepeca programme, Empowerment Coaching with young people who were emotionally, socially and behaviourally experiencing difficulty with some aspects of their lives. Four schools were selected.

Summary

Confidence, self-esteem and behaviour had made a notable improvement over the six/seven week period. All but one child (who was withdrawn from the school by their parents) that took part in the pilot achieved their goals and, in most cases, exceeded what they had hoped to achieve. There was no negative feedback from the children. The feedback from teachers was generally positive, however, it is important to mention that personalities and teaching styles (kinaesthetic, visual or auditory) did have an impact on the relationship between teachers and students.

Of 20 parents, disappointingly, only three returned feedback forms. Assessing individual children on their presenting issues and concerns provides options that not only suit that child's lifestyle but also enhances it. This in turn empowers them to use their inner resources to achieve and succeed with their problem-solving skills and thereafter their goals. Results are visible, profound and achieved over a short period of time. Client feedback was obtained by the coach.

Feedback Information

S********* Primary	3/3 teachers 5/5 children 1/5 parent
W******** Primary	1/2 teachers 5/5 children 1/5 parent
H******** Secondary	10 teachers 5/5 children 1/5 parent

S***** G****   0/1 teacher
Primary   5/5 children
                                0/5 parent

Influencing factors

Child's home environment
Cognitive development of child
Teachers/Student relationships
PlayStation / Xbox / TV / iPod / Nintendo – screen watching!
Bedtime and actual sleep times!

The following are testimonies from ESCO of pilot / parents / teachers / clients involved in the pilot: Testimonials are from both primary and secondary schools.

Conclusion

Empowerment Coaching is a viable option for children with emotional, social and behavioural issues and concerns.

Results are visible, profound and achieved over a short period of time. This was confirmed by the ESCO.

* * * * *

ESCO

"The impact of Julianne's work with students was swift and significant with parents calling to say what a positive difference Julianne had made to their child's emotional well-being.

From a student's perspective, Julianne's involvement resulted in a student feeling 'magical' after only six weeks' work.

From a school's perspective, Julianne's work was rated as the singular most effective intervention that the school had seen in several years.

Highly recommended."

*J** C** (Extended Schools Coordinator until Sept 2011)*

Mum

"X was so much more relaxed after you explained how to use the bubble. He was finally able to successfully ignore nasty comments from those who were bullying him. This is a 'priceless tool' because he always felt unable to laugh at the bullies in order to stop them. He is now also able to stop himself getting angry or upset. I can see him stop himself and he takes a step back and apologises if that is appropriate. He is more in control.

X is so much happier so we have all benefited at home with less confrontations and much more understanding. X was being bullied (for years) and had very low self-esteem. He felt he had no friends and was better off dead and it was very difficult to find out why he was like this and difficult to help. With coaching, he is so much happier and able to see things differently. He is now able to go to school without worrying about the others and what they will say.

He is happier and therefore nicer to be around and more people want to be with him. Before he just thought it would be easier if he were dead.

X still has his moments where he is not positive about himself. I think that seven weeks is not really long enough as his self-esteem was so very low. He has the tools to help him deal with things now but I am not so sure he is yet strong enough to keep them up. He needs them reinforced by a professional to keep him on track.

I would like to see him to be able to have a much more positive attitude about himself and to not underrate his achievements. I want him to become more confident. I think this can be achieved by more 'top-up' sessions targeting these issues. I hope that this may be possible.

I will be writing to the school headmistress telling her how very successful your work with X has been. It is lovely to see his true personality come out, which I fear could have been lost!

Thank you so very much."

Mum of Empowerment Coaching Client – 16/03/11

Mum

"From the very first session, I began to notice a difference in Z. The woman who was dealing with Z (I'm sorry, I forgotten her name) bonded with Z immediately, and Z was smiling and talking for quite a considerable time to me about the entire session.

Z enjoyed the sessions, the games and the encouragement she was given, looking forward to each week, and there's a noticeable difference in Z's outlook of situations and how she feels about different aspects of herself and others towards her.

We were going to Great Ormond Street at first to see a psychologist and, although this was okay, Z did not bond with the psychologist and we were grateful for your input with Z's problem.

Although Z has now finished her seven sessions and seems to be feeling much better now on being herself every day, I would be grateful if I could call upon you if ever Z lapses or feels the need for empowering. You would, in my mind, be the best help forward for her.

I would like to thank you with all of my heart. My daughter is very precious and you have helped give back that spark of love and light that you see again."

Mum of Empowerment Coaching Client – 16/05/11

Client Testimonials

Client

"I can walk away from fights. Feel better in myself. I noticed a difference with my friends because I won't fight so my friends are stopping fighting too.

I feel much calmer. My mum and dad are spending more time with me because I am calmer.

Empowerment Coaching was easy, fun and I learned new stuff.

I am trying to teach my friends what you did for me."

Client

"Empowerment Coaching has helped me control my anger and feelings.

I am not as agitated with things I find difficult. My mum and dad have noticed a difference. I use the RAG which helps me control my emotions and talk about things without getting upset.

Empowerment Coaching was fun, joyful and easy to remember. I would like to come here again if I start spinning out of control."

Client

"I don't take in as much what people say about me. I have been more happier since Empowerment Coaching. My teachers and my mum have noticed that I have been happier.

I am more confident and better in a way since doing this course. The bubble and traffic lights really help me.

I felt really down and had no energy but now I feel bubbly and more confident in myself. I look at things differently.

Empowerment Coaching was funny, helpful and interesting."

Client

"I found this course relaxing, interesting and helpful. I look at things differently. It has helped me sort stuff out. My mum and my brother have noticed a difference. I don't argue as much and I have stopped smoking. I know I can manage what I say and do. I can control stuff more; I realise how my actions can read and be seen differently by others. Empowerment Coaching was life-changing, made me more confident and helped me understand people, their actions and expressions."

Client

"Empowerment Coaching just helped. It was fun and funny.

I notice that I am not always in the head teacher's office now."

Client

"This course has helped with problems at home. Everyone at home has noticed a difference in me. I am more confident at home. I have got happier since doing this.

Empowerment Coaching is cheerful, non-demanding and exciting."

Client

"You are like Nanny McPhee – I want you to stay."

Client

"I feel like I have been saved – thank you."

Teacher's testimonials

Teacher

"X has been more able to listen to others rather than be heard all the time. He argues less and playtimes especially have been calmer. The class have benefited as there is less attention in his direction.

Thank you so much for a very valuable service. "

Teacher

"X definitely seems more secure with herself and generally happier.

Y is more focused in lessons and he is making more eye contact than before."

Teacher

"Empowerment Coaching has had a very positive effect on X.

She is far more confident and less likely to complain about minor problems. She is also more able to realise her part in the problem and do something about it, rather than ask for adult help. I feel X is far more equipped now to deal emotionally with her difficult life."

Teacher

"X listens to instructions and starts work without the need to be watched. She isn't as loud in class as she was before. She talks to me with respect and with interest. She has confidence to ask sensible questions.

Y is completing his work a lot faster and he seems happier in himself. He asks questions when he's not sure about something and participates in lessons."

Teacher

"I have noticed a real difference with X, Y and Z, and a great improvement in attitude from all three.

With X, at the start of the year he made inappropriate comments to other students, and it was a battle to get him to complete the work. Now, he works brilliantly. I trust him to sit next to another boy, he answers questions in class, and he tells me how much he enjoys history! Behaviour in lessons is good, he participates in the lesson a lot, and I definitely haven't heard anymore horrible comments to others.

Y and Z complete more work than most during lessons. Y especially finishes everything and then does the extension, whilst Z puts a lot of thought and detail in to her work. No behaviour issues from either (and I had a lot of issues with Z last year!).

I'm honestly really pleased with all three of them and now you point out that there has been this training, I can definitely reflect upon their behaviour and see a difference."

Teacher

"I had a word with X about how he has improved in maths and is more focused. The behaviour has improved immensely as before he used to shout out loud all the time and have a giggle over something very silly. Now he is calm and a lot more on the ball about his work.

I have seen a definite confidence regarding his work. He gives it a go and if he is really stuck, he will ask for help; mainly it's just asking if he is correct and he actually is."

Pilot Update 2012

A year later and the results of the Jepeca programme's Empowerment Coaching sessions are extremely positive as reflected in the student's feedback.

The update shows how students continue to find the Jepeca programme useful, empowering and practical. Enabling them to access the curriculum and further their education. Build their confidence, self-esteem and relationships in and out of school and make informed decisions with regard to their choices – present and future.

What the students say one year later

Client

"This programme saved my life. I am so different now. I am happy and love my life. I wish I could have done this a long time ago. My eczema has really improved and I no longer pull my hair out. Everyone at home treats me differently. I still use the techniques when I need too. Without this programme, I don't know what would have happened to me. Thank you."

Client

"I never argue with Mum now. I don't really drink as much as I used to either."

Client

"I have received 'Outstanding' in some of my lessons for the first time in my life – it's great! I am no longer disrupted in class and I am very pleased to be in Year 10."

Client

"I don't mind going out with my family now. My brothers can't help the way they are and I don't mind others staring because I know what to do. We all get on much better."

Client

"I have used the techniques from the Jepeca programme when I started in Year 7. They are working really well and although I miss my old school, I know I will like it here too."

Client

"I have more achievement codes than behaviour codes. If I didn't do this programme, I would have turned in to a lost boy. Thank you. Can I go back to class now?"

Client

"Empowerment Coaching really worked – but I am not sure how or why. I just feel differently about things. I know I can do anything if I put my mind to it."

Client

"I know I look different and it used to bother me but now it doesn't. I like it in Year 7."

Client

"I am not being bullied and I have friends. I am happy."

Client

"I have showed my mum and sister how to use the bubble. It really works - that is the one I use the most."

A total of 26 students that accessed the Jepeca programme from January 2011 were attending H********* Secondary School in October to December 2011. All students referred initially were unhappy and/or struggling with some issues socially, emotionally and or behaviourally. Some of the students providing updates accessed the programme after the initial pilot.

Findings were as follows in Dec 2011

Empowerment Coaching enables young people to achieve and succeed by teaching them various tools, techniques and strategies, both for problems and everyday life choices.

When young people know 'how to' think and feel constructively, rather than destructively, and filter what is being said, they 'can do' whatever they put their mind to because they know 'how to'.

The programme was and continues to be life-changing for many with regard to self-harming, coping with the death of a parent, attending school, behaviour (in and out of school), family and relationships, depression, bullying and maintaining their confidence, self-image and self-esteem. The Jepeca programme works.

It is fast, effective and measurable.

The Jepeca Programme

We offer six consecutive sessions, usually over six weeks, of fifty minute sessions during school hours concurrent with term times in an environment that the client regards as safe and familiar i.e. school or GP surgeries, social services etc.

We work on the client's agenda ONLY, although we do welcome information and details from family, school or other professionals to build a bigger picture. The weeks are as follows:

Session 1   Initial Assessment

Session 2   Filters

Session 3   Thought Training and Development

Session 4   Emotional Awareness

Session 5   Communication

Session 6   Final Assessment

"Her confidence and dealing with
peer pressure has improved.
She is more able to deal with difficulties
and conflict in a controlled and mature way.

She is much happier and settled.
We are very grateful for this programme.
We are delighted with her progress in herself,
her self-esteem, maturity and
confidence since doing Jepeca.

She is more settled in herself and at school
and although she is moving school,
she is not disturbed by this transition.

My wife and I are very grateful to the school
and the Jepeca programme. Thank you."

Session 1 - Initial Assessment

Week one is all about building rapport and information gathering. Boring, as it may seem to young clients initially, it is essential for us to step in to their world and get a sense of how things are for them. The more we hear, the easier it is to get a feel for how the client sees the sessions unfold. As they realise that the Jepeca programme is for them, about them and only them, their anticipation rises. As one young man put it ,"Nobody ever listens to me," and I replied, "Well, now they do."

We are conscious that some of our clients have previously been offered help to "make things better". They approach our intervention with suspicion and rightly so. We do not make promises we can't keep and we do not promise to fix anyone or anything outside of the client. Witnessing the relief on their faces that there IS something they can do to help themselves never grows old.

We have many forms, all of which tell a story in some way, shape or form. For example, we have the usual forms for insurance purposes, we have forms for the individual client to fill in, we have the form for after the sessions, the form for the commissioner of the service and we also have a unique questionnaire.

During the first session, we are under no illusion; the client is assessing us as much as we are assessing them. Building rapport is all about developing a relationship where trust and confidence leads the way to an experience that will benefit the client, both in the short-term and long-term. Without trust and confidence, the programme will not work and we would be part of the problem once again!

Initially, we start with their confidential information. It is interesting listening to the client hearing what they feel is important enough to make it on to this form! We have the usual name, age and date of birth, along with the address of where we are holding the sessions.

Then as we start to ask about bedtimes and actual sleep times, we watch them as their eyes widen in disbelief! "What you mean you know I don't go to sleep when I go to bed!" Shock horror. It is actually quiet shocking how long some clients stay awake, but not as shocking as the list, and I do mean list, of electronic, screen watching items in their bedrooms!

Most children these days will have at least three or more of the following in their bedrooms – television, DVD player, radio/stereo, iPhone, iPod, iPad, laptop, computer, Xbox, Wii, Nintendo DS or DSi or 3DS, mobile, PlayStation 1 ,2, or 3, portable DVD player, or some form of tablet.

The impact that these devices are having on schoolwork, amount of actual sleep and behaviour, in my experience, is massive. The video games that young people are playing are usually for over 15 years of age and, in a lot of cases, over 18 years of age. This can, and does, lead to inappropriate behaviour and very tired young people who find it difficult to concentrate – not a recipe for success! I have worked with children in Year 5 who are aged nine to 10 years of age that are playing games that were created for over 18 year olds. Somebody must be buying them for them! Where are the adults?

During the initial session, I ask that when they go to bed they go to sleep early – especially when they are working with me. I also ask them to stop playing any form of video games or electronic equipment for at least a half an hour before they go to sleep. They do normally comply with my request, which means I have their full attention and they are able to concentrate during our sessions, although sometimes I do get the odd apology as they admit to being on the games console too long last night and I appreciate their honesty.

From there, the clients usually think I have psychic abilities! Little do they know that almost every client has the same story when it comes to electronic devices in their bedrooms. Screen watching gets their brains active when they are in a place and time of relaxation and supposed sleep! A good majority of clients do not go to sleep until 1am or later because they are on some form of electronic device. In some cases, it can be as late as 4am. In all cases, their parents think they are asleep as they are in their bedrooms!

After that, we ask them about their family and, most importantly, their pets. It is important to know and understand who is who in the client's world as during follow-up session when they use this information in techniques, it allows us to concentrate on ensuring the technique, tool or strategy is working effectively, rather than figuring out who is who!

The family dynamics can be very complicated and this is displayed in the client's recall of family life. Some want to see their other parent or siblings or step-parents and step-siblings more, some less and some not at all. There are no hard and fast rules, no right or wrong answers; only individual lives and, for this reason alone, it is vital to get the information from the horse's mouth, so to speak.

A lot of clients only have pets to talk to and seek comfort from. When they are sad, lonely, angry or frustrated, they seek comfort from these pets. It is important to know what sort of pet it is, how old it is and, of course, their name. Clients always love talking about their pets and I always like to listen to them.

In one case, an 11-year-old girl used to talk to her rabbit when she felt lonely as she was being bullied in school. She had no siblings and her parents worked long hours so she didn't want to worry them. She thought that the bullying would stop when and if she ignored them.

When her rabbit died, her grief as well as the bullying got too much and she started to express her feelings in less constructive ways. Angry outbursts at her parents and her friends meant that she was more lonely and isolated which resulted in her feeling angrier, and so the cycle continued.

Her parents were beside themselves but after completing the Jepeca programme, she realised that only she could change her life, her circumstances and her behaviour. Happily, the ending for this girl is one where she has friends, is not being bullied, and has a good relationship with her parents - now.

The Client Attendance Agreement is a wonderful invention where the client can decide how committed they intend to be during our time together.

Each statement is to be signed and discussed, if necessary, until the client is satisfied with what they are signing up to.

Things such as attending every week with the right attitude, participating with an open and honest mind, asking questions to understand and voicing their opinion, are all part of the agreement. This allows the client the control over the sessions that makes the difference.

One 14-year-old client said he would find it difficult being honest to which I replied, "OK, that is not a problem, and thank you for your honesty." After a few minutes of thinking, he looked at me and smiled and said, "Maybe I can be more honest than I thought I could be!" Indeed. We referred back to that first meeting often during the six weeks.

We ask each client to put their thoughts down on paper by calibrating their confidence, self-esteem and behaviour. It always amazes me how honest and accurate they calculate these! They take great time and effort to ensure that the most accurate calculation is recorded. We also ask them where they would like to be after the six weeks. Again, great concentration goes in to thinking this through. Interestingly, very few want to be perfect. Most just want to be HAPPY!

The pièce de résistance is our unique questionnaire. This is always the last piece we do with each client, as by now we have a solid foundation with reference to rapport. The questions are divided in to different sections, which refer to different areas of their life. The Jepeca programme will be tailored to each client depending on his or her answers.

The first thing we do is read to them what is written across the top of the questionnaire, which is the following, "The questions are especially designed to help me to help you. There are no right or wrong answers but what I am looking or hoping for are honest ones (which has already been covered in the Attendance Agreement). Only you know how things really are, look and feel in your life."

This immediately allows them to relax and I get several comments at the part where I say there are no right or wrong answers! I also explain that the questions are tough, as they require some thought time, and are probably not something they usually get asked.... Now, for question one......

Q: Do you think your life could be better?
A: For 99% of clients, the answer will be YES.

Q: How?
A: Anything from wanting to get on better with their mum or dad, to doing better in school, to not being bullied, to not being the bully, to being better behaved, to not cutting themselves, to being happy, to doing their best in exams, to wanting to enjoy life, to wanting to have friends, to wanting to not fight, to wanting to be confident, to wanting to be thought of as a nice person, to wanting to not be shy, to wanting to feel better, to wanting to sort their eating out, to wanting someone to leave them alone, to wanting to be seen and heard.

Almost all want to manage their emotions and feelings, as well as have more confidence and self-esteem.

The list is endless, but a common thread shines through.

They all have the power to make it happen and, more importantly, want to make it happen.

Very few know how to manage their behaviour or emotions. Yet clients would like to behave differently and be in control of their behaviour. So, why is it so difficult for them?

Emotional health and well-being is talked about a lot these days but what is being done to educate the youth of today? Our adults of tomorrow? How can we expect anyone to control their emotions when they have not been shown how? Or when they see adults having difficulty managing their emotions?

We also ask clients to tell us three things they are good at, and this can be anything from brushing their teeth to rocket science. It is shocking how difficult it can be for some. With everything that they do on a daily basis, some struggle to think of anything they are good at! What does that tell us? How sad that, in their whole life, not one person had said, "Well done!" as in the case of a client I worked with. He struggled and, in the end, I said, "We can leave it for now," only to return six weeks later with a list as long as my arm!

Next, we find out if the client feels unique or special, or if they feel they deserve good things. The answer to this is mixed with some interesting answers. We ask them to tell us three things that are important to them, and again, it is interesting to note that the young people of about 14 to 16 who are displaying really bad behaviour in school rate their education as one of the three! That is why it is so important to us to get the view of our client.

Another thing we ask is, "Do you like being you?" It is very sad when the answer to this is, "No." It is even sadder how often we hear it! One such client had been experiencing such difficult times at home that she hated being her and was thinking about cutting herself or stopping eating to get her parents to notice her. Her parents were constantly fighting and shouting at each other and she didn't want anyone to know at school. After our sessions, she spoke to them and they didn't realise how upset she was or how loud they were!

The answers to the following questions give us a glimpse in to how the clients view themselves. We simply ask for three words that describe themselves. The answers range from some interesting and delightful ones to some of the following: sad, lonely, horrible, annoying, angry, ugly, fighting all the time, fat, useless, waste of space, stupid.

The hardest part of my job is listening to a person describe themselves with such harsh words. These are real thoughts and feelings being expressed by an individual seeking help. They just don't know how to change the way they are feeling and thinking, and that is where the Jepeca programme makes the difference. I know that in six weeks' time that will all have changed, so for now I just take notes and listen.

It is no wonder that their behaviour is alarming, because their thoughts and feelings are alarming too. It makes sense. If you don't feel good on the inside and you don't think good things, how can you display anything different on the outside! Six weeks.

Thankfully, once the truth is out and the initial session comes to a close, the planning and setting of goals for future sessions is our focus. Again, as with our entire programme, the client decides on what the next step will be. We usually have things like controlling behaviour, getting on better with someone, working on their anger, being less shy, getting better grades, building and maintaining confidence and self-esteem. Social, emotional, behavioural and academic goals are the most common but this is not an exclusive list.

The only thing the client has to have is a desire to change. We can do the rest. If, however, that wish to change comes from anyone else, the results will reflect this. You can lead a horse to water, but you can't make him drink – and this is also true for participating in the Jepeca programme!

As Jepeca coaches, we occasionally work with children who have letters after their name. I say that they have letters after their name as what letters they have will usually reflect how people deal with them. Labels, if you will. I agree that sometimes this can be helpful but, in my experience, it can be equally as unhelpful. The expectations of their ability have been set.

The letters could be OCD (Obsessive-Compulsive Disorder), ADHD (attention deficit hyperactivity disorder), ADD (Attention deficit disorder) or some form of autism, or they say they are on the autistic spectrum, or displaying tendencies!

What does that mean to us?

If the client can talk, think and feel, then we can work with them.

We have worked with some clients and we have been informed that they will not comply, or sit or listen, and that they behave badly, only to find this not the case. We take each individual as they come. We only work on the client's agenda, confidence and self-esteem, and if they do not want to work or change, then there is no work to be done. If they do, then six weeks...

The Jepeca Cycle

The Jepeca Cycle is a very simple and useful tool to help client's understand that if they always do what they have always done, they will always get what they have always got. Sometimes that can be difficult to verbalise so I use this every week to give a visual on what it is they are doing.

For example: As everything we do is linked to a cycle or reaction, it puts in to perspective where the change can be implemented and how the individual reaction can lead to a different outcome. If a client presents with bullying, stress, poor relationship with family or whatever you can think of, if you put in place the Jepeca Cycle, they can see that cycle and they can hear your voice confirm what they already know and see is happening.

One client I had used to shout and bang things when he got annoyed with his mother. By using the cycle, he could identify that it was not making any difference and the outcome was always the same. So the situation is as follows...

His mum would tell him to come off the Xbox.

His reaction? He would sulk, shout and then throw things, eventually pounding his way up to his room.

As a result of his reaction, his mum was upset and angry, he was angry and upset and banished to his room. The atmosphere was horrendous and he really did not want it to be like that. But he did not know how to change it. He also never realised that the cycle existed and it all suddenly made sense, although he still didn't know what do to change it!

He would eventually come back down to his mum and return to the Xbox. Communication would be restored but no resolution forthcoming until

Session 1 - Initial Assessment

the situation occurs again. His mum would tell him to come off the Xbox and so on.

The cycle continues until he actually reacts differently.

He loved that cycle and I used it every week to help him visualise how his actions, if continued, would give him a result he did not want. Another example was his reaction to the requests of his science teacher. Then I explain to the client that I will show him how to change the cycle so that he will get a different outcome, but he has to put the changes in place; I can only show him how to do it.

Remember, you cannot change anyone else, you can only change yourself. But when you change yourself, you influence the reactions of all those around you... and that is the difference that makes the difference :)

The ripple effect – remember the stone in the pond and how the ripples gradually expand to the furthest point? Everything in the way of the ripples will move or sway or change course to accommodate and adjust to this new wave. Remember, when you change yourself, you also change everything around you.

Here is an example of influencing others. Every day for a week, greet your friends or family in your normal way. Next week, greet your friends in a happy, cheery and fun way. Now for the following week, greeting them in a rude, obnoxious and standoffish way. It will not take long for you to understand the influence they have on people.... Amazing, isn't it?

I always allow time to process everything... Let the fun begin... After all, why wait? It is useful to mention that there may be people who refuse to change or move when you start to put changes in place. Generally, they have their own issues and I would usually just ask clients, "Why do YOU want to change?" And the answer is always because things are not working the way they are at the minute. Each of us has our own journey or road to travel and it is not up to them to decide or judge what the other person should or should not be doing. Leave that to the experts. After all, you can only change yourself; you cannot change anyone else!

"I felt I could be really open and honest
and talk properly.
I found the bubble really useful
and after the second session, the bullying stopped.

I can come to school now.
I am happier and smile a lot more.
I talk to my sister now
and we get on really well.
Actually, we are closer as a family.
I believe in myself and
used the techniques in my exams recently.
The bubble also helps when I have
nightmares about the bullies.
I know what to do now and understand so much
it has been really helpful."

Session 2 - Filters

Week two enables the clients to use their natural filters so that they do not absorb every negative comment or text. Life experiences are used to learn how to filter what others are saying, for example parents, teachers and other people of authority or peers. The focus here is on learning how to be proactive rather than reactive and for the individual's behaviour to reflect these positive changes. This tool is perfect for dealing with bullying, cyberbullying, psychological abuse and external influences, which can have a significant negative emotional impact.

> The sessions are interactive, apart from week one and week six.
> Every week is different. Every client is different.
> The anticipation for every week is generally the same.

One of the biggest differences between the Jepeca programme and other interventions is the buzz that follows each session, and I am not just talking about the client. The coach can calibrate the moment that particular week's session makes sense. Clients are usually excited to get using their new tools and techniques as soon as possible. They are also excited to come back for more.

Once we prove they have filters and the client is happy with the results, the next step is to ensure that will fit with their personality.

When they have their filters in place, we test that they are effective in filtering their issues, as it was designed to do! For this, we need experiences, situations and circumstances that the clients have lived through. In most cases, these will also be experiences, situations and circumstances that the client has found challenging. Clients will usually have many experiences to choose from and we look for the ones that have left a footprint, so to speak. One that we can trace, one that has not been resolved and has caused some form of block, which the client has found difficult to overcome.

Before we start, I remind them that there are many things that are real but cannot be seen by the naked eye. We explore examples together – the most common being love, air and words. Just because we cannot see something does not mean that it does not exist! The number of clients that will say that they do not have anyone that loves them is startling! This is where pets come in handy. If they do not have any two-legged people in their life who love them, perhaps we can find a four-legged one! If they do not have any pets, then I will find someone by including extended family, friends and, in some cases, teachers!

On one such occasion, a client had developed a close bond with his teacher. His parents were not in a position to offer support through his GCSEs as they were going through a challenging divorce. This for my client meant that he had to manage his exams, his living arrangements and his relationships with everybody at home. Sometimes when he went home, his mother would be crying and would then get angry. When he was with his father, he would hear snide comments on how it was not his fault that things 'fell apart'. There did not seem to be any support or thought for him as he stepped in to the unknown world of choices. Luckily for him, his school had noticed his behaviour was becoming an issue and referred him to the Jepeca programme; they had no idea what was happening at home but were more than willing to help. He felt unloved, unwanted in a way, and excluded from family decisions, whilst being left to look after his younger siblings whilst his mum and dad learned to adapt to the new situation. I am sure that you can see the irony of the above situation. Of course, his parents loved him (he did mention he had a great childhood until they decided to separate) but somewhere along the line, he became a casualty of his parents' decisions and choices. How he felt was real for him but not a true reflection of the situation within his family. By using his filters, he learned to ignore the angry words, unkind remarks and nasty comments. He formed a bond with his Head of Year, who supported him through his exams. He felt that he could rely on his Head of Year and at this point of his life, that was what he needed and so he felt as if he was loved. He also learned how to address his home situation so that he could make positive choices and decisions without being torn by the choices and decisions of the adults around him. He did very well in his exams with the support of his Head of Year and school. He did progress on to college and he and his family are now settled in a new and different life but one which he says he would not change as looking back, he knew his parents were not happy.

Cyberbullying has become more common of late. Bullying has been around for years, and for some, adulthood is just a continuation of the nightmare that was school. We cannot protect our young people 24/7 so it is vital that we enable them with tools and techniques, which they can draw on when needed. Many people and organisations have spent time and money looking at costs and statistics, so have a look at that chapter of this book for a clearer picture. Cyberbullying can and does impact lives just as much as verbal and physical bullying. In recent times, we are hearing of young people taking their own lives due to cyberbullying. This is unacceptable. Enabling and empowering young people is the way forward. Filters are perfect for verbal or written bullying as it is the individual's perception that leads to what will happen next. It is, after all, our psychological approach (how we think and feel) to the situation that will determine the outcome and course of action long before that situation becomes a reality.

Not everybody who comes in contact with a bully will circum to their agenda. One such incident that still makes me smile to this day is where a young lady was walking home from school and had been shouted at regularly. Now it would all be horrible and dreadful, apart from this young lady found the name calling funny rather than insulting (her psychological approach was one of amusement, not intimidation). You see, she was very tall for her age and a young man, who was rather small for his age, was calling her 'daddy longlegs'. She saw the funny side and, after a few weeks, he stopped shouting, as he was not getting the reaction he wanted and so he passed her quietly, as if nothing had ever happened.

One young man I worked with was receiving abuse on a daily basis on his way to school, at break times, lunchtime and on his way home. It was relentless. He was called fat, useless, and gay, as well as "Your mother" (which is a whole other story! Ask a young person to explain it) and a load of swear words, of which I am sure you can hazard a good guess.

What started out as "Should I, could I, say such things to an adult?" turned in to "If it's good enough for me, then it's good enough for you." How I deal with them is the difference that makes the difference – am I using my filters or not.

What is interesting is that the more fun and amusing the experience is the more honest and real the words and situation becomes. The balance is critical. Calibrating the client to ensure both effectiveness of the technique and understand of the instructions ensures the fun continues and learnings are embedded.

Now back to the filters... You control what you let in and out... So...

When I worked with Jean (again, a false name!), she was shocked to find that her bully felt so powerful. She couldn't believe how her feelings and understanding of the situation could be so different to the bullies. It didn't take her long to put her filters in place and not only see and hear, but feel the difference immediately. She grew two feet tall in that session, although I do not have the paperwork to prove this!

The realisation that the bully or significant other feels disempowered, annoyed, frustrated and/or angry usually surprises the client. The fact that the client can appear in control and calm also surprises the client. Win/win.

Then it is time for the client to experience how empowering using their filters can be, and so begins the journey that ends with a confident, empowered individual.

Using as many experiences, circumstances and/or situations as the client needs to understand and use their filters in a constructive way allows them the freedom to choose how and what they will do when the challenge arises.

I remind them that nobody knows that they have or are using filters. Some will teach friends, some teach their families and others like to keep it all to themselves for themselves. There are no right or wrong answers, only individual journeys. We are there to show them how to use their natural abilities to the best of their ability so they can live empowered, happy lives.

Filters can be used also to replay old movies or situations where they felt they could have been more empowered. The time lapse does not make any difference; it is how they recall the memories and the old feelings that are attached to that specific memory that will determine the next step. Using filters for old memories will allow the client to feel protected, safe and secure.

One such young lady I worked with cried the whole way through the first session – the initial assessment. I was prepared for the second session and brought some tissue. She did not want to talk or discuss the problem. This, thankfully, does not make a difference, as the result will always be the same when the client puts the techniques in place. On the second session, I was discussing her filters when she started to cry again. Tissues... I discovered that she was crying at least twice a day and often for long periods.

After allowing a brief moment to collect herself, I convinced her that it was important for her to go through the whole process to get to the desired end result. The change in her posture, facial expression and being is something I will remember for the rest of my life. As she began to understand the process, she grew taller, smiled and nodded. The change happened before my eyes and her brother was no longer an issue, and neither was the crying. Empowered, happy and in control. Sometimes it is difficult for the client to talk about, sometimes it can be difficult for the client to understand, but the end result is like putting in place the final piece of a jigsaw – the bigger picture is obvious and clear.

"I loved getting to have normal conversations
and feeling comfortable and very welcome.
My self-esteem has improved massively
and I dress how I want now.
I feel more comfortable in my own skin
and feel much happier.

The Jepeca programme really really
helped me to feel good.
I know how to improve my self-esteem
and confidence now.
My friends have noticed I am more confident
and talkative.
It was worth it, fun and helpful.
My relationship with my dad is improving
and he seems more comfortable with my sexuality."

Session 3 – Thought Training and Development

Thought Training and Development; you control the way you think. This is a week for exploring the power of thinking.

It is surprising how little people (no pun intended as adults do it as well) actually put in to thinking, considering we do it all day, every day.

Our aim for this week is to get the client to understand the process of thinking. Once they understand the process, they can make an informed decision on everything!

It is very interesting asking the young people to guess how many thoughts they have a day and what the impact of negative or reparative thoughts may have on their lives!

Once they have come to grips with the vast number and frequency of their thoughts, I usually ask them what they think they might spend their time thinking about? Starting from the moment they wake up in the morning to when they go to sleep at night, including any and all negative thoughts.

Frank was one such young man of 12 years old. He hated school and would always begin his day with some thoughts such as, "I don't want to get up", "I hate school", "Why do I have to go?", "Why can't it be the holidays?" etc. etc. Every morning he would say the same things to himself and his feet felt like concrete, as every step he took was more and more heavy and tiring.

As we went through this session, he began to realise that he was not helping himself. He decided that for the next week, he was going to adapt a new strategy. Together, we used the thought training and development technique to put in place a more positive workable solution.

The following week, Frank appeared for our session with a huge smile on his face. He had a great week and found getting up in the morning much easier. It is all about the way you think of things. He had also used his thoughts to get one of the top marks in his class – another first.

The first step to getting anything done is very simple. Yet when asked the question, what would your answer be?

What is the first thing you need to do to actually get anything done?

Let's just explore that for a second. If your thoughts stay in your head, then that is all they will ever be...thoughts.

Good, bad, mad, ridiculous, happy, sad, angry, adventurous, murderous, playful, nasty, helpful, honest, dishonest, daydreaming of lands far away and flying with your new superhuman powers to get there, or receiving an award for being the best at what you do, or providing humanity with the answer to world hunger, peace etc. These are but a few that spring to mind. All are thoughts with the potential of becoming real or not. The first thing you need to do is to decide what you want to do, and then just do it.

Your thoughts become more real the more time and effort you put in to them. That is a good thing – really! That means that the more time and the more effort you put in to making your thoughts a reality, the more real they will become. Simple, but true. Your time, your effort, your result – you decide.

Simple and to the point. Everything you do is a step to making your thought a reality. A step in the right direction, so to speak, and if you change your mind at any point you can just change direction. As with any other thought or desired outcome!

One of the reasons young people give for not achieving or succeeding is that they do not have any money. Money is NOT a factor. How you think about money is a factor though! Putting time and effort in to what you want to make real, is a factor! Money not so much.

When the clients get the idea, I usually stand back and allow them time to absorb what we have done. I invite comments, thoughts and questions and observe the response to my answers. Interestingly, they notice the change straight away. The steps are always within their abilities and capabilities as they decide what they are. They really do have the answers within.

Whether the clients want to understand and trace the steps that brought them to where they currently are or design a future of their choosing, is not important. What is important, is the process. Understanding the process allows the client freedom, and freedom allows for choice that leads to informed decisions for future outcomes. Repeating negative thoughts can also make for a reality that leads to low confidence and low self-esteem. This is a fine line that is very easy to adjust once the process has been identified.

The commonest negative thoughts that have the greatest impact in my experience are, "I can't," and "I am stupid". There are many more but, for the most part, these two stunt the growth of many wonderful, exciting and fun plans or potential adventures.

Amazingly, of all our thoughts, most can be stunted with the previous negative statements. For the most part, young people will freely admit that once they think they can't, they will not even attempt the task at hand.

I could have said try but that word in itself implies that it will fail. Either they will succeed or they will not, either they will do it or they will not, they will behave or they will not; there is no grey when it comes to try.

Once the individual realises how it all works and how they are providing the negative messages on a daily basis and repeating them on a regular often daily basis, the cycle becomes clear. Then the solution is simple.

Once the client recognises that their thoughts are as random and unpredictable as the weather (well I do live in the UK!), but their power to develop and train specific thoughts is as simple as one, two, three, it then becomes easier to ensure that the positive thoughts are what they want and that the negative thoughts are dealt with as soon as they are noticed.

Training the client's thoughts and developing them has a massive impact on confidence and self-esteem, exam results, future plans, interviews, emotional health and well-being, making friends, dealing with bullies etc.

In fact, everything you think of starts with a single thought and only develops if and when you decide to put time and effort in to training and developing it.

Janice was a secondary school student when I met her. She had very low confidence and self-esteem due to her past experiences and family life. She preferred to spend her time alone. She had often been seen walking to school in winter with no coat and her clothes were often tatty and smelly. This led to bullying from her peers, and so the cycle continued.

When we worked on her thoughts, it became apparent that she did not see the point of taking care of herself or her clothes as nobody liked her, which was ironic as one of the reasons people did not like her was because she did not take care of her hygiene or clothes! She was also deeply saddened by her home life, and this left her little energy to take pride in her appearance.

As she learned to train her thoughts, she realised that she repeated a lot of the same negative thoughts on a daily basis. In fact, she had very few positive thoughts. This upset her for a short time but with the dawning of a new reality comes the empowering realisation that she can be and do whatever she wants.

Janice controlled her thoughts and took the necessary steps of training and developing them when she realised what she was doing. It was all her choice and she enjoyed the control. Confidence and self-esteem are no longer an issue for her. Nor is loneliness.

The best thing about the Jepeca programme is that the changes are all within the control of the client. If the steps are unrealistic then the client has the power to reassess and reconsider the desired outcome, put it in to their own words and understanding and take the necessary steps to achieve it. They decide how, what and when. We work on a conscious level and so the client becomes master of his or her own destiny – literally.

Our jobs as coaches are to show them how it is done and guide them in the process until they are familiar with the steps. Their reality and journey will be reflected in their choices. I have yet to meet someone who wants to make bad choices or who wants to hurt people without what they believe to be good reason.

As Janice said, "It is easy when you know how."

Now you know. Take the steps to make your reality a happy, productive reflection of your choices. Or not, you decide. Go to it. Make it so.

Just a note on thought trees.

Now if you were to expand on a thought to see where you could go with it, it would look something like a tree. Every step is a step in the right direction, leading to another reality of your choosing. The possibilities are endless as are the choices. Branches lead off to smaller branches to twigs and eventually leaves.

Some of the steps may be towards long-term goals, whist other steps towards short-term goals. For example, John was confused about what he wanted to do as he approached his exams. As a 16-year-old, there were many choices ahead of him and the more he thought about it, the more confused he felt. By using the reality tree, he felt more in control of his destination. He felt more clear about the steps he wanted to take, and if he had the desire to take those steps. Sometimes spending years at college or university is not the answer. Again, that is for the individual to decide – not me!

Reality trees are helpful to understand how each step has the potential to develop, such as your behaviour, choices and consequences of those choices, or to reflect on where you have come from. They are a train of thought that has developed or has the potential to develop but can change direction in a heartbeat.

Just a note on cycles.

Cycles are a great visual way of getting the client to see the impact of what they are doing. By repeating the cycle they are stuck in until I can see that recognition on their face, ensures that the full effect of the repeat cycle is being understood. From here, they can change how they behave and that in turn will change the final outcome.

Depending on the client, I may use the cycle on every session. If I feel that they are stuck in the same behaviour or thought pattern, then it is really effective in getting the point across.

Session 4 - Emotional Awareness

Emotional awareness is such a huge subject. For many people, they do not care about being aware of their emotions or feelings, they just want to stop feeling sad, bad, annoyed, scared, emotional, upset, horrible, angry, frustrated... The list could go on...

When working with teenage boys on emotions, I would imagine it would normally be received with, "Do we have to?" or "Here we go." But because the Jepeca programme has been unpredictable and fun (not my word – one of the most commonly used words to describe the Jepeca experience), up to now the mention of emotions and feelings normally gets, "OK," which, in the land of teenagehood, is no bad thing!

The idea with emotional awareness is for the client to understand and utilise their feelings in a positive and conscious manner, empowering them in the process. The reality in society today reflects the ever-growing lack of understanding and knowledge with regards to such a simple common useful tool.

With the Jepeca programme, we are awakening the powerful knowledge and intuition that takes refuge in the vast unconsciousness of our minds, which await recognition, acceptance, acknowledgment and appreciation. Emotions and feelings are probably the body's most overused misunderstood gifts. This week, we work with the client to enable them to understand and control their emotions and feelings.

Once understood (feelings and emotions), the beauty of their simplicity enhances the quality of experience, and enables prompt, efficient results, time and time again.

We break down the negative association clients usually have with feelings, especially if there is an issue with anger or managing their temper. They realise that feelings are normal, necessary and not the issue or problem. It is what they do with them that make the difference.

One chap I worked with spent ages thinking of all the different feelings he had, in alphabetical order... That was one long day but very effective for the client. It was his way of making sense of emotional awareness.

At the end of that session, he told me he enjoyed our time together as nobody usually takes time to do the things he wants to do. Fact. So by listening to him, he felt happier, and by understand emotional awareness, he now knows how to maintain that feeling. Win/win.

In the Jepeca programme, we do things differently so that the individual can make the difference they want to see in their lives easily and effortlessly (apart for putting in the time and effort to get their desired result obviously!). And so the cycle continues. There is no lost cause, just endless opportunities; it just depends on the choices you make which will determine the end result as to what happens next.

I always ask the client where they spend most of their time feeling wise? The answer to this question is often heartbreaking. The amount of young people who are operating in a negative space continuously is frightening. They just don't know how to change things to make a difference.

I can see the clients thinking of different situations in their life where they did not listen to their feelings and emotions. Allowing them time to absorb the process, and process the process, is really important. Once they understand 'how' it works, they then have the ability to develop and use the process as they wish – job done.

The energy we use when we are really angry cannot be sustained for long periods of time. Thank goodness, I hear you thinking. I always mention that if and when they get really angry, they WILL always come back to a calmer state. There are good and not so good points to returning to that calmer state though. It is just as important to address the choices available during their time in that calmer state, as it is the emotions and feelings that have got them there in the first place.

What they are currently doing when they come back down to a calmer state is choosing the same behaviour, action or choice, in exactly the same or similar situation. If they were to make a different choice, then everything else would change as well, so the outcome would be different.

Remember, feelings are giving you a chance to change your world, but only if you act on the signals you are receiving. That is what we focus on next - how to access choice when the signals are telling you that you can change your world if you so desire, or risk losing your temper for a short period of time. But if you do lose it, you will always come back to a calmer state where you get a chance to change it all again.

Remember the cycle I mentioned earlier in thought training and development? It is important to return and enable the client to address their emotions using the exact same cycle. For example, by using the cycle with the client during emotional awareness, you can assess how the last session went and remind them that they have the power to make the break or change as and when they decide. Remember that with the situation, there are other people involved and as you can only change yourself, your reaction is the difference that will make the difference.

Our motto is, "Use it, don't lose it".

Usually, I will ask them if they know what losing the rag means? Surprisingly, quite a few do. Hence, use it, as in use the RAG, rather than losing it, makes perfect sense. If the client has not heard of it, they now know something they didn't know before, and so continues the session. And if you have not heard of it, losing the RAG is when you lose you temper.

The RAG starts with what to do when you feel you have lost it, so that you can regain control and address those neglected feelings that so desperately attempted to get your attention. Failing their attempt at the subtle hint that you should make a change, your feelings accumulate and they give the full blow force of many emotions all at once.

Now you are forced to address the fact that something has happened but, for the most part, people get so caught up in their actions, they again forget to address the feelings behind those actions and the cycle continues.

Using the RAG will allow you to gain a perspective that empowers you to take action on the choices and options that will work best for you.

But first, as us humans tend to do with a crisis, situation, problem or issue, we spend time, effort and energy talking about it... Why, why, why? Telling me how troublesome it is, why it affects their life, what they can't do because of the problem etc. etc. etc. Want to talk some more? Off we go again. It is because I can't see a way forward and I don't know what to do and it stops me doing this and I don't like it anyway. Not only do we talk about the problem but usually it is in a negative way!

Are they done talking yet? Seriously, some people like noting more than to talk about the problem and issues. They get so much sympathy and attention from having the problem that if they were to change, lose it or get rid of it, their lives would be unrecognisable.

That is a scary prospect for some people, especially adults! Young people for the most part want to change but just don't know how. They are trapped in a world of adult rules and regulations that many adults do not conform to. It often amazes me that people are quick to notice bad behaviour but not the reason behind it. Nothing happens without a reason. Look beyond the behaviour and you will find the reason. Now you can do something about it :)

Someone has taken steps that impose a reality on to young people that they are unable to deal with and sometimes responsible adults ignore. This is an almost impossible situation for a young person and as they do their best with what they have at the time, life and life experience is not in their favour. They rely on the adults to provide structure and safety. Young people need to be applauded for their actions. They know what is happening is not right and are not willing to put up with it. The problem is that their actions, be they internal or externalised, are not working and the situation remains the same, as does their reactions and outcome.

One young girl was living in a house where her older adult brother on a regular basis was physically abusing her. Her older brother had learning difficulties, and when the parent went out, she was supposed to stay in her room for safety! She had to share her bedroom with another brother as the brothers could not share, again for safety reasons. She was so unhappy.

Everyone knew about this – school, social services, police, but nothing was ever done about it, even though she complained regularly that she was not happy in her environment. The head teacher was extremely supportive and had many an anxious hour wondering what to do with her situation but no other professionals got involved.

For this young girl, adult rules mean she has to do what her elders say. Adult regulations mean that she has to attend school daily and be in the care of a responsible adult until she is 18 years old. Confusing, isn't it?

The reality imposed on her by the steps that her parent and sibling take, impact on her everyday life, as do the steps that professionals do not take.

We can all think that something should be done about such cases, but if all we do is think, then we are staying in our heads. Remember we have to get up, take action and do something, take the steps, to make a change and make something real. It will break the cycles that are already in place that do not work, and thereafter, if the result is not what you want, just make another change. Sorted.

Think of people who have the ability to make a change, but want to stay in the situation for reasons only known to them. Believe me, this happens more than you think – especially with adults. I would like you to become aware how, as adults, we have the power without the restrictions, unlike young people. What we do with it often gets lost in a haze of problems and issues. We are the voice of young people, we have the experience and we have the knowledge. We need to wear our underpants on the outside and use our powers for good, just like Superman! Stand up and be counted.

One man (adult) I worked with was very depressed. In fact, he had tried to commit suicide twice. Things had got so bad that it was decided among the extended family, for his safety, that he would live with his elderly parents. When I arrived on my first visit, I was greeting by his mother, a wonderful woman with a kind, concerned, yet caring, face. She guided me into her sitting room and scurried off to the kitchen to get tea and biscuits.

During the first session, the initial questionnaire, I soon discovered the benefits that this client felt he had from living with his parents. His responsibilities since his wife died were now the responsibilities of his extended family. His children, in their late teens, rallied around his every need and had postponed university and college to be on hand as needed. He actually told me in that first session that he liked his life the way it was and that he would work with me only because his family wanted him too.

We discussed what he wanted to get out of the sessions and, apart from feeling more energetic, he told me little else was needed. I returned one more time. On the second session, he told me that he had thought about his life and what he wanted as the questionnaire had prompted him last time. He said he knew what he was doing, so much so that he had in fact planned his last suicide attempt for when he knew his sister would be visiting him because he didn't like living alone since his wife died and he loved the fact his children were there for him whenever he needed them. I was flabbergasted!

That was the end of our sessions. You can bring a horse to water, but you cannot make them drink. If the client does not want to change or recognise that they need to change, no intervention will be of use. Last I heard, he was still the centre of his world and, many others' as well.

I do believe it is important for us to hear ourselves saying out loud exactly what the issue or problem is. Counselling is a useful talking therapy that allows clients to do just that, to talk in a safe environment about their problems and issues. Admitting that whatever is happening is not currently working takes courage. Once we acknowledge that what we have been doing is not working, it is time to move forward. Change, however, comes from a different, separate and conscious acknowledgement that YOU have to change something, no one else can. One of our clients enlightened me with his version of the difference between counselling and the Jepeca programme, which I think is spot on: "In counselling, I talk about my feelings, but with the Jepeca programme, I know what to do with them." It describes perfectly how the Jepeca programme works with regards to feelings and emotions.

A client soon realises that you can talk all you want but nothing will change unless the cycle is broken and action is taken. The part that will change everything is the reaction to the situation.

When faced with a feeling, the reality is that many people do not stop to think what it could possible mean. Or even what the possible outcomes could be.

By using the RAG, it is possible to identify and recognise the feeling or feelings, associate those feelings with a specific situation or situations, and then make an informed decision.

This may sound complicated at the minute but remember we work with young people from the age of nine years old and they have no trouble processing the information. In fact, we very rarely get asked questions, although I do get the odd personal question, like do I have a cat or horse or lizard!

Before we address these signals, we have a discussion on how anger gets a lot of bad press. By that, I mean that when people get angry or show anger, they often get in to trouble. It is, of course, what they do with their anger that is the problem, but for most people, the actions that follow the angry feeling will be their reaction in the cycle of similar situations.

It is often said that people have anger issues, or they need anger management or as many young people say to me, "I have anger problems." I find this very sad. Anger is just a signal. It is giving a message about a particular situation, which is not acted upon and eventually the person loses it. But how can a young person know what to do with anger if they have never been taught!

If nothing changes, when the situation arises again, the anger will return and the signal will communicate, but if nothing is done, the cycle continues. Feeling anger is no more or less important than any other feeling, it is what you do with it that counts.

When they realise that anger is in fact doing a wonderful job of signalling to them that they are not happy about the situation and something has to change in order to return to a happy, calm and relaxed state, it makes a huge difference.

This week works well for all feelings or signals. Regardless of the situation, it explores the choices and options that are available. The key is to let the client choose what would work. It is no good coming up with a list and then telling them, for example, to speak to their parents if they do not get on with them or are not living with them! The point is to empower them, not tell them what to do. There are enough people doing that already and it is NOT working.

Put the client's future in to their hands and let them see how much of an impact their actions have on it. Let their choices make the future they dream of. The majority of young people do not realise how their feelings can influence their decisions. Some do not even realise they have feelings. Even less of them know what to do with them.

We have a lot of fun during this session. It completes the Jepeca programme. By the end of this session, the client can see the whole process. No matter what happens, they are in control of what they let in and what they let out by using their filters. They are in control of what they think by training and develop their thoughts to work for them. The client is control of what they feel by acting on their feelings or signals in a manner that will get results.

We have empowered, happy, productive, in control people. Mission accomplished... nearly!

We look at the whole programme as it is on the board. It is very important to let the client absorb what has just taken place. A lot of very personal information will be visible, as will the outcomes that the client thinks will be effective and get them results. The cycle of events is also visible.

Very powerful.

The thought tree is also present and shows when steps are taken. Each reality can develop in to a branch of the tree which shows past, present and future choices and options. Their life, they decide. As the tree grows, they can shape their future.

I also have the reputation wave on the board. With this, the client is aware that they could possibly have a reputation, especially those who have misbehaved or displayed behaviour that has been worrying or challenging. Interestingly, they know that they have a reputation and, by seeing that, they have to ride the wave until they reach the shore; they can see that it will take a little while.

If they fall off the board (programme), they can get back on again and catch the next wave... there is no rush. Their classmates are on the shore enjoying their relaxed ability to misbehave without the sharpness of the teacher.

The clients understand that they are treated differently to other classmates. When I explain the reputation wave, it all makes sense. Again, it is one of those no lose situations. No matter what happens, the client is always able to regain control; if, of course, they want to!

One 10-year-old client saw the reputation wave and suddenly realised the reason his teacher would get annoyed with him and treat him differently. He was disruptive in class and had developed a reputation, which had followed him from the age of six. His parents had separated around that time and he found the adjustment difficult.

The fact that he saw the others being naughty occasionally and getting away with it would make him misbehave even more. He recognised the cycle straight away. After that, he decided what he wanted to make a reality. He put it in to the reality bubble, got up and started to take steps to make it his reality. By week six, he was enjoying school, especially his playtimes with his friends! But, most importantly, he was behaving in class and accessing the curriculum.

Session 5 - Communication

The focus this week is on communication, internally and externally. It is important to understand how communication works. After all, if we cannot communicate with each other, how do we get our point across and interact with others? Also, if we understand how things affect us on the inside, we can communicate what we mean effectively on the outside.

I start by asking the client what communication means to them. The reply is usually the same – it is how we talk to each other. These days, Facebook, Twitter and BlackBerry Messenger is also categorised as a common means of communication.

Now would be as good a time as any to mention that for many young women, problems and issues mainly stem from the means of communication that influences and often rules their lives, which is Facebook, Twitter and BlackBerry Messenger. There are many others that constantly change with the times.

The number of young girls I see that are experiencing bullying, victimisation, loneliness, sadness, isolation and/or low confidence and low self-esteem is shocking. In fact, so popular is this form of communicating that news spreads not only from school to school, but nationally and internally in a heartbeat.

This was evident when I was worked with a few girls individually in one school over twenty miles away from where a very serious incident happened in another secondary school. These girls had all sorts of personal details, information and finer details that had happened to the girl in question, names of suspected bullies, what had happened, how it happened and what was to happen next! I was surprised at the speed of communication, but what was even scarier was the lack of truth in the communications. Not one girl questioned whether the information was correct. In fact, there was no bullying but that did not filter true.

Drinking, smoking, drugs and sex (applies to secondary school children namely), partying or socialising is also common among many young women. Much of the alcohol and cigarettes is bought by the parents in a hope to monitor the amount consumed! Being accepted and appreciated for who and what you are, is difficult as a teenager. Even more so if you do not like what you see in the mirror.

Boys are a different kettle of fish in some respects but similar in others. Football and gaming - playing games consoles (electronic devices) and fighting for status and recognition - are the main issues and concerns we notice. Lack of confidence and low self-esteem are also very common issues. I am always impressed at how honest and precise young people are at calibrating their confidence and self-esteem.

Gaming is considered communicating, as there is a feature that allows you to communicate with others as you play. The quality of communication though is very poor. The level of communication is at a bare minimum and the tone of communication is often questionable. Boys as young as nine or 10 years old are playing games recommended for over 18 year olds. So what age are the people they are communicating with? Who knows, is the answer!

Just a thought! Finger pointing does not help anyone. Parenting is challenging as it is and not for everyone. There is no right or wrong way to raise a child. It is, however, wise to consider that, as young people, their experience is limited. Their knowledge is limited and their perception of what is, is reflected by these limitations. Yet despite or in spite of this, they know when something is not right and when something needs to change.

There is so much more to communication than just words. This is the perfect opportunity to explore how it impacts on the client's decisions, choices and options without them even realising it.

By going through some examples of communication with the clients, they soon begin to get the idea. I also point out that cyberbullying consists of words and that is the smallest percentage. Albert Mehrabian's findings on the elements of communication are as follows and widely used:

Words	7%
Body Language	55%
Tone	38%

The client's behaviour is what others always notice and comment on, but this is just the symptom. What is really going on? This is what we do as Jepeca coaches. This is where we work. The reason behind the obvious is where the answers can be discovered. Yet for the most part, people focus on the impact of the obvious, not the reasons behind the cause of the impact.

It is nearly impossible to hide your true self. For the majority, something in your communication will disclose your real feelings, thoughts and opinions. When I listen to clients, they always tell me what I need to know. By listening, I can hear their tone, words and observe their body language for confirmation of congruency. It amazes me how many times people do not hear what they have just said. Often, I will stop people in their tracks and get them to repeat what they have just said – and then they are amazed as well.

If our bodies provide their own natural therapy, and our behaviour has a positive intention, then perhaps the focus should be more on directing that positive behaviour to reflect the direction we wish to take? Using our thoughts to take steps, our feelings and emotions to signal we are moving in the right direction, and our words to reflect what we really think. Just a thought! We have 92% positive change with what we do, so it is working.

Problem solving is also covered in this session. We are all comfortable talking about our problems. Maybe not discussing the problem with everybody, but certainly with the chosen few. For some, this can become a negative cycle resulting in getting nowhere fast!

There are three parts to dealing with an issue or problem that we find will change the client's perception. Each part is powerful and well received, delivered with a sense of fun and assessed without persecution.

Once, when I was exploring a problem, my client said, "But I don't have any problems now. I know how to use my thoughts and feelings to sort it."

It is important to have the client understand that if and when things do not turn out as they would like, it is **feedback** to them that something needs to be changed. The more time and effort they put in (to the best of their ability) to things, the better the result. They will get a different outcome each time they change even the tiniest of details. Change one thing and everything changes; try making a cake and adding vinegar!

Feedback is an accepted part of schoolwork, coursework and desired information on a given project, topic or other as an indication to the person of how well they are doing. However, interestingly, this changes when I start talking about tests, exams, driving tests that they have not done well in. Even the terminology changes to incorporate the word 'fail'.

Failure is the client's perception of a set of circumstances. It is still feedback, but often gets mixed up with being a failure for not succeeding. I remind them that if I attempt to make a phone call and it goes through to voicemail, then I have failed to make the call, but does that make me a failure? Or if I miss the bus, elevator, start of a film, or I'm unable to make a party, does that make me a failure? It is all in the way we think about things. Make your thoughts work for you. Be honest, be real, be happy and, most importantly, be you.

Did you fail the exam, or did you not put enough time and effort in to revising, practising? There is a degree of honest needed with oneself here. To the best of your ability means that you have given it your best. I worked with a young man who struggled with his ability as he was achieving low scores and doing his best. This required a trip back to thought training and development where negative thoughts impact his confidence and self-esteem. Your choice, your time, your result!

I also use examples such as a driving tests, brain surgery, teaching, flying planes, dentists or other areas where the difference between feedback and failure, although the same, can mean very different things. If we did not have such measures in place, we would be endangering our lives with below par drivers, surgeons, dentists, pilots or teachers? Perish the thought!

Although doing your best is important, equally is setting a standard to recognise when a person is fit to do a job properly. It does not take long for someone to recognise that they do not want a person who does not know what they are doing to fly a plane, perform a filling or drive a car!

Once the clients realise that feedback is there to let them know how they can improve, if they wish, it is, at the end of the day, just the opinion of one person (who, although is usually an experienced person in a specific area, will be influenced by their experiences and history in the field).

If we have time, I like to get the clients to do a recap of the last six weeks. As each of our sessions are very different and packed with empowering information, tools, techniques and strategies, it is interesting to discover which part the client remembers and uses.

This is also where they get the chance to retrace the steps of the last few weeks and process the programme. If there is an area, which does not make sense or if they are confused about one of the sessions, this is a wonderful opportunity to readdress and clarify things.

How they recap is also down to individual preference. Some like to draw, some write, some sing, some act and some like the plain old-fashioned talking. There is no right or wrong way, just a way that works for them. I really enjoy the different ways that the clients bring the programme to life.

What surprises the clients most is the fact that the programme is simple. There is no homework. There is no pressure. Time goes by so quickly, and yet they are able to recall the majority of the sessions easily and effortlessly. I also get a chance to see which techniques they use and which they do not.

Another thing I've noticed on my journey is that a number of young people like to fiddle. They like to keep their hands busy whilst still learning and absorbing information. I always take them as they are. I am not there to change their personality but to enable them to change it if they wish. From some of the feedback I get, I know that this has enabled them to relax and be themselves. Feedback such as, "Non-judgemental", "I can be myself" and "Fun" is used regularly.

During this session, I like to awaken the expert that is within each of my clients. From the day they were born, they were communicating and to this day, they are able to walk into a classroom or their home and tell immediately who is in a mood, who is happy, angry, sad, wants to be left alone, loved up, listening, daydreaming etc. And that is exactly how the teachers can tell too!

As I say each sentence, I notice how the client is recalling past situations where this may have been true. Their eyes look up, or their gaze almost seems to look right through me as they take a few quiet minutes to run through their thoughts in peace. Eventually, when they are ready, I brace myself for what, nine times out of 10, becomes a tornado of questions that leaves no stone unturned.

The awareness they now have removes the initial awe and wonder of my amazing psychic abilities! It means that they too have a magic of their own – and that is empowering.

Session 6 - Final Assessment

Week six is one of the most amazing, emotional weeks of the programme. This is the week where the client and coach evaluate the effects of the Jepeca programme. It is, in fact, a very important week. In order to progress, is it necessary to process. This week allows that processing to be a conscious observation. The progress the client feels or think that they have made over the six weeks is written and recorded, word for word, exactly as they have experienced it.

Sometimes the difference the clients make are blindingly obvious, whilst at other times, it may appear subtle to the observer, but life-changing to the clients. For example, being able to speak up in class, or put your hand up to ask a question, or take part in the school play, may not sound life-changing to others, but for that individual, their whole world has just opened up.

We repeat the question of the initial questionnaire and record their answers, noting and discussing where appropriate the difference. Often the client does not even notice or remember what they were like only six weeks ago!

Although we bring them back to the way things were mentally, we do not linger but rapidly fast forward to where they are today, noting the differences in the way they think, feel, behave, and any other observations or areas where they have noticed changes.

Things like, "I am not in the head teacher's office now," or, "I am getting on much better at home," or "I just feel happier," all contribute to the overall picture. Remember, it is how they think and feel that got them in to this non-productive cycle in the first place, so understanding how it all works enables them to think themselves out of (by utilising the signals from their emotions and feelings) situations, environments or circumstances in the future.

We have included some feedback, which we have received over the life span of the Jepeca programme. I wish you could witness the effect the techniques have on the clients. Only the other day, I worked with a young girl who was hysterical and talking about suicide whilst in school. She was brought to the attention of the staff during a lesson, as she was distracting and beginning to hyperventilate. As I was in the school, I was asked if I could help. Of course, if I can, I will, so I did.

I had got a brief handover from the staff, concerned that she had been coming down regularly and the situations and her behaviour were getting worse. She had been to counselling twice before and they were going to put her name down again as they did not know what to do with her.

I asked her if she wanted to speak with me and spend some time together and she said yes. When we got to a quiet room, I started to tell her about me, what I do and how I do it. She was really interested and had stopped crying. I noticed her state/mood change over a short period of time.

When she was calm, I discussed the cycle. As she nodded and confirmed that she needed to change something I asked her when she had started feeling this way. To this, she answered last September or October. Without going in to detail of the initial events, I asked her what upset her the most at the minute. It became apparent it was her thoughts.

The way she was thinking was not serving her well. She had a voice telling her to do horrible things and she was worried that she may do what this voice was saying someday. The voice was getting louder and, as it got louder, so her behaviour got more worrying.

Over the next hour and a half, I discussed thought training and development with her, as well as touching on emotional awareness. To this, she commented, "It is like you are inside my head." I assured her I was not. As she began to turn her negative thoughts around, she began to smile. She did not realise that she had so many thoughts or that she had the ability to train and develop them, if she wished.

So many times, I hear the following: "I didn't know I could control how I think," or "If I think about everything, I could change everything." YES, now go for it, and enjoy the journey, step by step, with an outcome or goal in mind. Never has it been truer; be careful what you wish for! What you spend your time thinking about is what will become. Simples. We think all the time every day, even daydreaming is thinking. If you want something, think it in to reality.

After our session, she was booked in by her secondary school to attend the full Jepeca programme. She felt much better by the end of that session and I know that the breakthrough she had that day has changed her life forever.

She will still benefit from the full programme to understand the way it all works but she sat in awe of herself and her thoughts and their ability to develop by her spending time just thinking. That would have been a wonderful session to record to capture the Jepeca programme.

That is what I wish you could witness. The sheer despair, hurt and desperate plea for help that is so often heartbreaking. She did not want to be this way, but she did not know how to change it. This applies to most of the young people we work with. They do not want to behave the way they do but how can they be different if they do not know how?

She said whilst she was attending counselling that she felt OK as she could talk about her problem, but as soon as she had stopped, it all come back again and now it seemed to be getting worse! That, in itself, is a cycle!

I was not surprised. We work with a lot of young people who are offered and/or attend counselling, some who have been attending counselling for many years. For some, it may be helpful but for many young people, it is not. For some schools, the fact that they have a counsellor in place is a box ticking exercise! Many of the young people we work with refuse to see a lot of professionals because they have been in and through the system so often and still feel the same.

A lot of young people complain about having to sit and talk about their feelings. Feelings are **NOT** the problem. They are a signal. They are just doing their job. Well done them, I say. It is what you do with them that make the difference, not what you say about them.

Remember what one young man said (and I use this a lot to describe the difference as this young man who had experience of both explains it perfectly): "In counselling, I get to talk about my feelings, but with the Jepeca programme, I know what to do with them." Knowledge leads to a freedom that only those in the know are aware of!

To complete week six, we offer the people who interact with the client the change to give feedback i.e. parents, teachers, SENCOs etc. The feedback we receive has been overwhelmingly positive. The difference this programme is making to people's lives is evident.

We have empowered young people who are now happy, in control and productive. I am sure all of these young people will impact the world in a positive way with some going on to make a significant contribution to mankind. It is often the brilliant that have trouble fitting in with the ordinary.

As a result of the Jepeca programme, we have found that the referred clients can swap roles in situations by choosing a reaction that will benefit them long-term, at home, at school or with friends, and behaving in a mature way often reversing roles when adults behave like children. Especially true for those where life has become a struggle or challenging.

For example, when teachers are making fun of, shouting at or ignoring a young person in front of the class and they use their filters withholding their normal reaction, which is being mature? When parents say hurtful things, when they are preoccupied by life's troubles and strifes, bills, work, relationships issues, death, dying, old childhood unresolved issues or when they are unable to be present and provide a stable, safe and secure upbringing for their child for whatever reason, who is being the adult? Who is being the child?

I do believe that people do the best with what they have at the time. I also believe that people are born good, and want to love and be loved. However, somewhere along the line for some poor souls, their hopes and dreams become blurred or extinguished by life's challenges, and this influences what could have been with what is. I have worked with such people in my previous life and this trail of destruction is altering the course for our next generation. It has to STOP.

An empowered, happy and inspired, young person understands that not only are they responsible and accountable for their own lives, but they have a real impact and influence on the lives of those around them. Just beautiful. Mission accomplished. :)

The following are a small selection of case studies, which I hope will give you a glimpse in to the benefits and, in some cases, miraculous turnarounds experienced by young people completing the Jepeca programme. I am very proud of our clients and what they have achieved, and I am also very proud of our Jepeca coaches and what they are achieving, on a daily basis. Names, places and dates have been changed to protect their identity.

You can refer back to the Jepeca programme in the first part of the book by using the appropriate week, as mentioned in the case studies.

> Empowering people is our passion.
> Inspiring happiness is what we do.
> Happy, in control and productive is what we get.

The hardest part of writing the next section was selecting the clients! 92% of the clients we have worked with make positive amazing life changes and we feel privileged to have been part of the process that enables these changes to take place. We love what we do, but remember, it is just the beginning...

Enjoy!

"Her behaviour was under control
as she used the RAG regularly.
Most importantly, she really liked being her
and had lots of plans for the future.

Sam mentioned that she found her spark
and felt more confident."

Case Study Number 1

By Julianne Hadden

Reason for referral from point of contact in school

Sam   16 years old   Girl   England

Sam was referred to the Jepeca programme as she had problems at home. Most teenagers could claim to have some sort of problems at home, like no privacy, always being shouted at, not enough pocket money, too many jobs, annoying parents, boring weekends, always being told what to do or what not to do, but for Sam, the reality goes beyond the norm. Neglect also played a huge part of the worry and concerns by the school.

The truth was that, behind closed doors on a daily basis, Sam endured a constant torrent of abuse that slowly ate away at her confidence, self-esteem and self-belief. This constant slow drip of verbal abuse resulted in Sam's behaviour providing the best support it could under the circumstances. Sam looked sad, drab and grubby. Her clothes were always dirty and her hair looked messy. She had nits, which went untreated over a period of time, which, in turn, led to issues with her peers!

Social services had been involved previously, and the family was at various times under scrutiny due to referrals by professionals throughout Sam's childhood. Malnourished, failure to thrive and lack of discipline were some of the concerns. Although social services were no longer working with the family, the concerns that the school had were still in place. Sam had very low self-esteem and did not make eye contact.

The point of contact from the school informed me that she was a bit of a loner and was often seen with her head in her hands in what appeared to be despair. She did not talk to people and had been attending counselling previously, which the point of contact said made little or no difference.

Sam always looked very sad and she looked odd. When I asked her to explain what she meant by odd, she said to wait and see for myself. She seemed to draw attention on herself by the way she dressed and had experienced bullying. She thought Sam might have been self-harming but, when asked by the point of contact, Sam declined to answer.

There were serious concerns for Sam's well-being, welfare and safety.

Session 1 – Initial Assessment

I was not sure what to expect when my session with Sam arrived. I began by offering her a seat and telling her about myself, who I am and what I do. This allows her time to relax and check me out, and her surroundings. I noticed that as she looked around the room, her appearance was indeed different. This was interesting because, although she was being bullied for the way she looked, she did not change her appearance or try to fit in.

Rapport building is very important when working with clients. If we do not have rapport, our sessions will break down very quickly. During our training, we spend a lot of time exploring the different ways in which we can get in to rapport quickly.

For example, when we first meet clients we will observe their body language, listen to the tone of their voice and to the words they use. We get a feel for their mood, and this gives us a picture of how they perceive themselves. By using the same type of language and words that our client's use when we talk to them, they begin to feel comfortable, which allows us the ability to access their world comfortably. If you try to answer someone in a different tone to how they spoke to you, the results will be interesting – try it! Bet you will not be in conversation long, but it is fun if used in the right environment!

We use the first session for questioning specifics within the world of the client to get a bigger picture or, more specifically, the client's bigger picture. In this case, Sam's world and Sam's bigger picture. Another important rapport skill, which is highly effective, is listening. If you listen, you will hear the answer, or answers.

Listening is very effective when done properly, but its effectiveness is questionable these days, because in order to listen, we have to focus on what the other person is saying totally without interrupting. How many people do you know that do that? How many people listen totally and completely to what you are saying?

Listening and rapport have many strands and many advantages, which allow us to provide the client with a feeling of being heard and being accepted. If we do not have trust, if we do not have rapport, then we are doing our clients an injustice. Clients come to us for help and to find answers. And we succeed in providing these 92% of the time.

Now back to Sam. For Sam, I realised from the handover from my point of contact that she had much intervention with little evidence of change so it was very important that she felt safe, secure and comfortable in what would become our Jepeca space over the next six weeks.

I explained what we would be doing over the following weeks, starting with today's session. As she processed what I was telling her, I noticed that she began to relax, just a little, but just enough for me to observe her physical appearance.

She looked very sad. Her shoulders were hunched and her clothes looked a little grubby. Although this was in line with previous reports to social services over the years, I could not be sure at this stage if it was because she was not being looked after at home, or if she had little pride in her appearance.

I noticed that her eyes lacked spark, and when she spoke, her voice was low and flat, as if even speaking was draining her energy. Her hair was greasy and had bald patches where she had pulled out her own hair. There were dry patches of skin on her face and hands, which looked very red and sore. It appeared to me from her nervous behaviour, avoidance of eye contact and by listening to her use of words that she was in distress and wanted help. She would say things like, "What is the point?" "I hate my life," "I don't like being me," "I am ugly," etc. etc. etc. Very sad and difficult to hear, but this was Sam's reality.

After I explained the format for the weeks, Sam was eager to continue with the programme, as she could see how and where it would help her, so I began the initial questionnaire. On answer to my first question, "Do you think your life could be better?" Sam replied, "Yes, if I stopped pulling my hair out." She was not happy and did not feel safe anywhere. When I asked her where she felt happiest, she said a particular place in her local park, where nobody goes, overlooking a pond. She really preferred being on her own.

Although it is important to take time to process information and experiences by oneself, it is also necessary to be able to socialise. It became apparent that Sam felt she could not trust anyone in her life currently and so felt it was safer to be on her own. Her socialising had diminished to such that, apart from attending school, contact with people was non-existent. Something I have noticed with young people over the years is that the more upset, sad, hurt, annoyed, angry, frustrated they feel, the more isolated, withdrawn, insular and untrusting they become. At the final assessment, their world widens. Where they feel happiest changes, as does who they like to spend their time with!

Sam didn't believe in herself or like being her. She liked the fact that she was different to others, in the way she dressed and her hobbies, but at the same time, she struggled with her body image, confidence and her self-esteem. She had no idea that she had feelings or emotions, although she did recognise that the way she acts and what she does (pulling her hair out) caused a lot of tension at home. By listening to the words she used, she had given me the answer to her most pressing issue – she was not aware of her feelings and emotions! How could that be possible in this day and age – but she is by no means the only person to proclaim this.

When it came to her family life, Sam went very quiet again and looked away to a corner of the room. She understood that I needed the bigger picture and was speaking even lower than before. Her mother and father were separated but worked together in trying to make her stop pulling her hair out. In fact, they had been trying for many years. No matter what they did, Sam would continue to pull her hair out and, in fact she said, the condition was getting worse. The worse she felt for letting her family down, the worse her condition became.

It had got to the point that Sam was beginning to control what she ate. Again, this is not exclusive to Sam. Where there are feelings of no control, an individual can pick on something they can control, such as weight, self-harm, or pulling hair out. This gives a way to control a part of them that is providing a natural therapy, which is the best they can do at the time, but is not beneficial to them long-term.

Sam said she felt ugly and fat and it felt good to have some control over her life. The more her parents wanted her to stop and the more they did to make her stop, the more she resisted and the worse her life appeared to get. She felt she was going around in circles and nothing was ever getting solved! She was tired of it.

Depending on whose house Sam was at would depend on how and what they would do to stop the cycle. Her dad took a more psychological approach, yelling and shouting that she should be in a psychiatric hospital, saying that she shouldn't be near normal people with the way she behaves. He did not want her near his new family, as she was a bad influence! This upset Sam greatly as she loved her stepbrother and sister but was never allowed near them.

Her mother, on the other hand, took matters in to her own hands on several occasions by shaving her hair over a number of years to teach her a lesson. Driven by frustration and unable to change her daughter in the way that she thought would be better, the damage slowly took its toll on Sam. The school and social services were also aware that this was happening but Sam remained within the environment, becoming more depressed, withdrawn and different.

At times the disclosures were so upsetting that Sam would just sit and cry. Then she organised her thoughts and when she felt ready, she would continue recalling how life was for her as she sees it. How she felt being separated from her step-siblings and the impact it had on her life to date.

I was not surprised that her behaviour was an issue!

I always tell my clients that they are coping unbelievably well in their situation. I tell them that I am not surprised that their behaviour is as it is or that they are doing what they are doing. I tell them that I think they are doing a great job. This is not something they hear very often.

There is something in letting them know that I accept them for who they are and what they are doing that appears to free them and allow them to move forward to find a new way of doing things that will work in a more positive way.

The first issue I wanted to deal with was how and when she pulled her hair and eyelashes out. When I had an idea of what her life consisted of, I had an idea of how and where she could put the techniques in to place over the next few weeks. For now though, it was imperative that I get a technique in place that Sam could use when she had a desire to pull her hair or eyelashes out.

I asked her to remember the last time she pulled out her hair. I wanted her to mentally recall the situation, where she was, who she was with, what was happening. What was it that was driving her to physically pull her hair out? I asked her to remember the very first time she did it. Interestingly, most people can identify the exact (or roughly to the nearest) moment when their issue or problem started. What was happening around that time? Were you happy with the outcome? She mentioned that she noticed that she was always at home and usually after an argument with her mum or dad (when at her dad's).

Then I asked her to think about the situation she was in. By think, I mean get her to realise that she is thinking. As thought raining and development will help her to address how she chooses to develop her thoughts, I wanted her to begin to realise that she goes through a process, the fact that she has the ability to choose the outcome will come later.

As she recalled the details, it became obvious to her that there was a point when she realised that she was pulling her hair out. From there, I asked her to think to herself that this part of her deserved to be heard. When we explored what it wanted to say at that time, she said that she was frustrated. That part of her was frustrated by her lack of control over her life. After all, if she were to think it through, it was her natural therapy for the situation and environment she found herself in, even it if it was not actually helping her long-term!

She found this an interesting way of looking at things. The ability to recognise that she was thinking about it and the fact that it was actually trying to help her made her feel better. If that part of her was actually trying to help her, then it was important that she listened to what it had to say. So from there, I asked her to keep a diary. To give a voice to this part and allow it to say what it wanted, when it wanted, as nobody would ever get to read it.

Sam loved this idea and thought long and hard about what she would call this part. In the end she decided she would just call it RED, as that was how she felt (interesting, as that would fit in nicely with our week five emotional awareness session). Excitedly, she left her first session with a plan; she had began her journey of empowerment.

Session 2 - Filters

By week two, Sam had begun to put in place a voice for RED with great effect. She mentioned several times how amazed she was that RED was frustrated, hurt and lonely. But this was not the week to explore her emotional awareness and so I listened, encouraged her to continue with verbalising RED and continued with session two.

During this week, Sam enjoyed the fact that she could remain respectful to her parents, yet not absorb the hurtful, hateful and unhelpful comments. I used the technique to hear what her parents were saying to her, and the aggression and anger in her voice as she delivered the words was interesting.

Reacting as she usually did, Sam could see how it worked from different perspectives. She also found that by always doing what she always did, she would always feel how she always felt. This refers to the cycle, which allows the clients to put a visual on their current patterns. By listening to the words she said and the images those words conjured up, she could link them with specific feelings, which led to specific behaviour.

So the only way to get something different was to do something different. By doing this, she saw how by changing her reaction (putting in new words and new images of what she wanted, it would produce a different feeling and a different behaviour of her choosing) and using the bubble, she could get a different result, one that would help her feel good on the inside. She was amazed at how empowering it felt. Her smile let me know that it was working. She grew two feet tall that day.

We used several situations and experiences so that Sam had a thorough grasp of what and how to use the bubble. Some of these situations were from past experiences, and some from the future. For example, in the past, she would have experiences with her peers, her mum and her dad and his family. With reference to future situations, Sam knew she was to stay with her dad the following weekend, and at some point, he would 'start on her' about pulling out her hair. I used this to provide her with the experience before the event for the future event. After each situation, I let her process what we had done and ask questions, if needed. When it came to the end of our session, Sam told me she was looking forward to using the technique and reporting back next week.

I reminded her that the more she used the bubble, the less she would need to use it. Strange, but true. I also reminded her that she would experience this before the end of our time together. Already I had noticed that she was smiling more, holding her head up when she talked and had maintained eye contact for the whole session. The progress she was showing came just two hours in to the Jepeca programme. Just two sessions! Sam was happy and enjoying the sessions, and so was I.

I would later learn that it took two days for Sam to put in place the bubble so that any remarks from her peers and especially her family would not infiltrate her core. From that time on, Sam used her filters successfully.

Session 3 – Thought Training and Development

I knew Sam would find all of our sessions useful but this week in particular was very exciting. I knew it would play an important role in her internal dialogue and the impact thereafter would be reflected in her confidence and self-esteem. As it was, I had heard from staff and the point of contact that she looked more confident around the school and she was actually with friends at breaks.

As I began the session, Sam talked excitedly about the last week's success and about her dealings with RED. She was still pulling out her hair and eyelashes, but was also putting in place the ability to give that part a voice, in a more useful and acceptable way that she could be at peace with. She had noticed that she was becoming conscious now during the hair pulling activity, and that was progress. Then she would stop pulling her hair out and realise that she was having negative thoughts, which was her cue to stop what she was doing and start writing a journal of the thoughts and feelings of RED.

By conscious realisation, Sam was becoming aware of the thoughts and feelings that she had during the process of pulling her hair out. She was then able to communicate those thoughts and feelings in to a tangible journal and give them a voice.

As we worked through the thought training and development session, Sam was surprised that she had the ability to choose the thoughts she wanted to work on, and even more surprised that she could take steps to make those thoughts a reality. When it came to negative thoughts, Sam was shocked at how many negative thoughts she had, but very happy to hear how easy it was to change them.

We worked on some mantras that she could use to replace the negative thoughts she currently had. This took a little time, as Sam did not like herself, in any way. Initially we looked for some words that she could say to herself which sat comfortably with her. It would have been too much of a jump for her to say something like, "I love being me." In the end, she settled on, "I am me," for this week, with a view to gradually building up to, "I like being me," and finally, "I love being me". Homework for the week sorted.

The rest of the session was spent explaining how it all worked and how she could change and use her thoughts to make things happen, or not! She still had the negative thoughts but she was in control of whether she developed them. She loved it. Once again, she left the session on a high, which rubbed off on me. She also left with a plan to make plans for her future, which she was very happy to know she controlled.

Session 4 – Emotional Awareness

Sam walked in to this session with a smile on her face. She was using her new techniques for issues at home, but also at school. She had not been bullied since she put her filters in place. Her mother, and her father when she was in his house, were still saying inappropriate things to her, but she was able to use her bubble and her journal to work through it.

Sam found the RAG very useful. She had not realised that she had feelings until she went through the programme and did not know what to do with them, or that she could do something with them. Feelings are signals, and as young people become conscious of their emotions and the gift they bring to their life and experience, they begin to understand the importance of them. Several times she mentioned that she has been frustrated for such a long time and nobody had helped her until now. But, of course, now she knows what that frustration was a signal for and the options that were available to her.

As we went through the different situations and circumstances where she felt different emotions and worked through each possibility, she realised that she always has a choice and should she decide to do something about the situation, she also has a lot of options available to her. As I watched her, I noticed that the darkness that was evident on her first visit had disappeared. This was not the same girl.

With every session, I could see an improvement in her overall appearance. Her pride in her appearance changed. She still dressed different from her peers, but her clothes were clean and fresh. Her body language appeared more confident. She spoke clearer with good eye contact. I could see her on occasion taking her time and thinking through before answering as she processed her thoughts and considering her options. Her options were not only considered internally but she felt safe and confident to discuss openly with me. Feedback from my point of contact confirmed my observations.

Session 5 – Communication / Recap

I checked with Sam on weekly basis about her progress usually by asking, "What was the best thing that happened to you since I saw you last?" and, "What was the worst things that happened since I saw you last?" This allow me to gauge where I should start the session. Usually, as the weeks progress, there are more positive things than negative reported. It is as if the more empowered they become, the more their circle of trust expands.

Because of Sam's circumstances, I wanted to ensure that she understood how we communicate and, as she was worried about her parents, how this also applies to her parents. I could tell that the techniques were working well for her as she was much more confident as the weeks progressed, but I felt it would be beneficial to her if she could relay to me (and herself) all she had put in to place over the last five weeks.

As she stood looking back at the work we did in this session, she mentioned that she understood why her parents had done what they did, but also that it had not worked. When I questioned her on this, she said that things were changing around her because she had changed herself – just like I had said it would.

I had the deputy head teacher approach me to compliment me on the change that his staff had noticed with Sam about the school. She was mixing with her peers, contributing in class and walking around the school corridors with her head held high. She did not appear to be in despair and was seen with friends before and after school.

I can only show people how to use the Jepeca programme, but it is ultimately up to the clients to want to make the changes. You can bring a horse to water, remember!

Session 6 – Final assessment

The final assessment appears to come all to quickly. The amount of hugs and, "Thanks…" for showing clients how to use their life skills to the best of their ability is humbling. I love my job. I love what we do, but I love week six for the feedback, which enables clients the ability to become aware of the progress and shift they have made in such a short space of time.

Sam's journey was particularly memorable. She is a bright, talented and unique individual who had momentarily lost her way. On her last session, she brought with her a beautiful picture that she had drawn especially for me and a warm hug, which was gratefully received. As I mention to all clients at the beginning of our programme, my job is to show them what to do and then for them to put to practise how they see fit. Our time together may be short but the gifts we leave with each client are permanent.

On Sam's final session, when asked if she thought her life could be better, she answered, "Yes, but I now know what to do to make it better." She was happy and felt safe. She was happiest at school and had many friends now, who appreciated her for who she was and what she brought to the friendship.

Her behaviour was under control as she used the RAG regularly. Most importantly, she really liked being her and had lots of plans for the future. Sam mentioned that she found her spark and felt more confident. She was more cheerful within herself, and her friends and teachers had noticed a difference in her behaviour. She said she didn't feel like a freak now.

Describing the Jepeca programme as life-changing, empowering and fun, the most powerful statement she made that day was the fact that "life was a chore before but now it is more enjoyable".

A year after Sam completed the Jepeca programme, I revisited to update the results. Sam was looking so different when she came for her session. She was happy and smiling the whole time. She was doing very well in school and her home life had changed totally. She had a relationship with her mother that she enjoyed, and her father and his partner and family enjoyed having her over for visits as well.

She also mentioned that she no longer pulls her hair out and that her skin had cleared up. She believes that the stress she was under had been responsible for her bad skin. I could see that her hair had grown back and she had a new haircut. She still used the techniques that she had learned in the Jepeca programme as and when she needed to. She no longer kept the journal for RED but had intended to keep it for some point in her future. She had put weight on as her diet had improved and was no longer obsessed with food or controlling it as she had spent a lot of her time planning social events with friends.

She was really enjoying her life, and had many plans for the future and her education. I received another hug that day with a recommendation to bring the Jepeca programme to all young people who were experiencing challenges in their lives. As Sam's life continues to unfold, she has the ability to make the changes that she wants to make in her life, and I am very happy to have met her.

"I felt really down
and had no energy.
Now I feel more bubbly
and more confident in myself.

I look at things differently."

Case Study Number 2

By Julianne Hadden

Reason for referral from point of contact in school

Linda   15 years old   Girl   England

Linda had very low self-esteem. She was seeing a counsellor and psychotherapist, and had been for a number of years. She had been self-harming for a while and was seeing the GP but the fact was that it was getting worse. The cuts that had once been well hidden on her upper legs had now started to appear on her arms as well.

Both her parents were worried sick about her behaviour and the fact that she always seemed sad and was becoming more withdrawn as time passed. They had done what they could when they could but the situation remained the same. The fact that Linda was able to hide her sadness from most people by her bubbly personality did not help. She appeared to be the life and soul of the party and was part of the popular gang within the school; a position only obtained by having a presence and street cred that was desirable. The plot thickens...

She had a visible disability, which she found hard to cope with. There was no more information from my point of contact on this disability. There had been the normal sort of problems at home. I use the term 'normal' loosely as what exactly is 'normal' and who exactly is 'normal'? We all have an individual story to tell, a road to travel and a life to live, so 'normal' is probably the most inappropriate word to use, yet it is the most identified word when explaining what we take to be the 'norm'! Linda was the middle child with two older sisters, who did not live at home, and two younger bothers, who did. They were a 'normal' middle-class family. So, what was going wrong? Her parents were extremely glad of the input, help and support that was been offered by the school.

The staff loved Linda and had tried everything to get her engaged and involved in school in the hope it would build her confidence, but to no avail. In fact, her attendance was beginning to become a serious issue. Her parents were worried sick and were ringing the school every other day for inspiration. The timing was perfect. Jepeca was providing Empowerment Coaching, and Linda was lost, sad and lonely. It was decided that she would be an ideal candidate to participate in the Jepeca programme.

The time, date and setting were set; now we waited to see if she would actually turn up. As I sat drinking my morning coffee with my point of contact, I could almost hear the ticking of the clock as each second that passed represented a step closer to what I later found out was to be a life-changing experience for Linda, her future, her parents, her siblings, her friends and the school attendance records!

Eventually, three and a half minutes late, Linda arrived at the door, full of life and energy. She eagerly thanked my point of contact for the referral and we headed to our room to begin.

Session 1 – Initial Assessment

My first impression of Linda was one of a girl that was part of the 'populars'. The populars are a group of male and female students who grace the school with their presence. They usually travel in packs and can be perceived as 'stand-offish', 'better than' or even 'the wannabes'. Of course, that is not the case, but on talking to other students, it appears that many people want to be in the populars. The reality is that, on an individual basis, each of the populars are just as 'normal' as the rest of us!

Linda was so very charming. It was so easy to see why the school was desperately trying to save the wonderful qualities of this girl from slipping in to the abyss. She was polite and smiling, and very pretty. She was, however, plastered with an inch of make-up. Every time she came to see me, she had to pass my point of contact's office, who would tell her to remove her make-up. Every time, she would remove it, and every time she returned, she had the make-up on again, and so the cycle continued.

I found it amusing and it appeared to be a sort of bonding experience between my client and my point of contact.

Behind Linda's eyes was a whole other story. Our sessions are private and because we only work on the client's agenda in private, we are in a privileged position. As I explained who I was, what I did and how I did it, Linda was absorbing her surroundings, including me! The rapport building had begun and as the session progressed, Linda's guard was dissolving inch by inch (just like her make-up, once seen by the point of contact). The question was, would it be enough to get to the crux of the problem?

As I started the session and progressed through the paperwork, Linda began to realise that I was actually going to be working on what she wanted, not what the school wanted, or what her parents wanted. This, she mentioned, was refreshing as there had been times in her past where she was told what was going to be worked on, which she did not think was an issue. I also checked to see if there were tissues in the room as many of our first sessions contain tears, make-up disasters and free-flowing fluid from the nostrils, or in some cases, all three! Nothing phases our Jepeca coaches – we are ever ready! :)

As I approached the initial questionnaire, Linda was sitting back in the chair, sipping on her water and had dropped the smile she wore on the way in. Behind the smile was an interested, beautiful and scared, little girl. Now, I thought to myself, we are getting somewhere, but where? I noticed that she had leaned over and brought the tissues closer, in anticipation of what was to come. Not too long to wait now....

I started with the first question: "Do you think your life could be better?" Silence...

Finally, Linda looked me in the eye and started speaking in a slow, meaningful and deliberate way. "Yes, it could be better. Much better."

Next question: "How?"

Not so long to wait this time...

> If I didn't have to go to hospital
> If I was pretty
> If I came to school more
> If I didn't fight so much with my mum
> If I didn't go out partying at the weekend
> If I did my homework
> If I had longer hair
> If I had a 'normal' body
> If I didn't cut myself
> If I wasn't ME!

There I had it. The floodgates were open and Linda was crying so hard that she found it difficult to see where the tissues were. I know this because she knocked the box of tissues off the table as she reached for them. I sat and listened. Now and again, I would ask her if there was anything else. She hated everything and everyone, but most of all, she hated the way she looked and that was why she cut herself. She thought she was fat and starved herself in the morning and at lunchtime, but by the evening she was so hungry, she just ate and ate. Trouble was, it was whatever she could get her hands, and she lived near a chipper! (For those in the need to know, that is a fast food restaurant that has chips as one of the main dishes!)

When Linda was finished, I asked her the next question. "Are you able to make your life better?" This was not something she had thought of before. I know this because she said so. In fact, she said that this was not something that she has ever been asked before. So, was she? Was she able to make her life better? The answer to that was, "No!" There was no surprise in her answers, but there was in her face as she heard herself verbalise her thoughts and feelings.

I studied her reaction and I noticed that as she heard herself say things, probably for the first time, she would look down and go very quiet for a time. Then as and when she wanted to involve me again, she would look up as if she had suddenly become aware of what she specifically needed to do. It was soon going to be time to choose something to do about the things she wanted to change and the challenges she faced, and that was where the Jepeca programme comes in.

She also discovered that she did not like being her; she did not know how to keep the darkness that hovered over her on a daily basis at bay, and she really did not like being her. She felt happiest in her bedroom by herself. As her world continued to close in on her, the more unhappy she became, the more she isolated herself. One vicious circle, easily recognised by using the Jepeca Cycle, which is what I said to explain it to Linda. Her eyes widened with recognition.

The unhappier people become, the smaller their world becomes and, as is evident in our questionnaires, the answers of our clients reflect this time and time again. For Linda to feel happiest in her bedroom, she had by this time stopped talking and discussing things with her friends, family and even her pets! She used to have two cats. One, she loved dearly and called Mac; the other, not so much as she was a tad wild and was named Socks. Unfortunately, Mac was getting older and Linda felt as if she was soon to be totally alone.

We progressed through the questionnaire, and at the end of it, I told Linda what I could do for her. I could show her how her filters worked so that she would not absorb negative comments. Even though she was part of the 'populars', Linda was very wary of the comments that people carelessly threw around, and although she was good at hiding the fact that she had absorbed them in public, in private the evidence was plain to see on her arms and legs.

I could show her how to train and develop her thoughts so that they would be productive, rather than destructive. This would impact on the way and what she thought of herself and how she could change it if it was not working for her. Her confidence and self-esteem would benefit. It would also help her with her homework and planning her future.

I could show her how to recognise and use her feelings and emotions to be productive, rather than destructive. This would help with the self-harming she was currently doing to herself. She had mentioned that it makes her *feel* better and she *feels* like it releases some pain and takes the focus on her problems. I could show her how communication works.

By the end of that first session, Linda was excited. She was smiling and she was feeling what she described as a buzz. Not only was she looking forward to the next session, but she told the point of contact on the way out that she really enjoyed it and felt so much better already.

Although I mentioned that Linda had a disability, I did not ask her the details in this session. If she wanted to talk, then so be it; if not, I could wait. Most of the people Linda had spoken with through her life had focused on her disability. I did not think this was the issue but it was how she was thinking about it that was. It may very well have been part of the reason she was experiencing difficulty at present, but Linda was, and is, perfect the way she is.

We need to hear ourselves say things out loud, as if to affirm what we think or what we believe. Once what we are thinking or feeling has been released from our minds, hearts and thoughts in to the atmosphere, we are free. After all that happens to a feeling once it has been recognised and acknowledged – that is right, it disappears until we need it again. We can acknowledge it or hide it away, but it will be heard either verbally or physically. Remember, the body will always provide its own natural therapy, and in Linda's case, this was self-harming and experimenting with food. From there, it's about finding a way to move forward, or choosing not to.

You live until you die, so why not make it a happy journey?

Session 2 – Filters

For this session, Linda arrived early, and so we began. But not before my point of contact provided wipes to clear the inch of foundation! It became a standing joke before each session – did she make it though!

As we started in to the second session, I could see that Linda was absorbing, listening, thinking, feeling, processing, every bit of information. We used some of her real-life experiences so that she could understand how and where it would work in her life.

The experience that we used was an incident where she was walking down the corridor in school and some random girl started staring at her and whispering to her friend. Linda could hear the odd word but could not make out what exactly was being said. She mentioned that she felt really annoyed and hurt when people stared.

From here, she started to discuss her disability for the first time. In her mind, she was made incomplete, not a whole person. This, of course, was also confirmed by the reactions of others staring, commenting or laughing. Linda went on to explain that she was born with a condition called Amelus. I had not heard of this before and asked her what exactly was it. She explained that she was born without an elbow or forearm and one of her legs was also disproportionate in size.

I could see that Linda knew loads about the subject and was genuinely pleased that I was showing an interest. So we discussed this for a while and when she came to a natural pause, we used this example to demonstrate how her filters and her bubble would work to protect her. Of course, it is human nature to observe and that can occasionally be seen as staring. So when it came to me being her and her being the person staring, I banged things, tripped up and laughed out loud. Of course, I knew Linda would look so I shouted, "What are you staring at?"

It worked perfectly. Human nature, you can't beat it. Curiosity is a natural instinct and one which has kept us alive and out of danger for millions of years. Just because we look does not mean we are being rude. I have used this before with another boy who had a sister that had additional needs and hated going anywhere with her because she used to shout all the time. Once he realised that it is human nature and a natural thing to do, it changed his experience with his sister and their family outings. Instead of shouting at people, he used to smile and say, "It's OK, she is my sister and that is just how she is." He found people were so much nicer to him!

Linda worked through a few more example of where people were staring or where she received texts with the word 'freak' in them, and each time she would use her bubble effectively. I could see the smile on her face as she realised that she controlled what she let in and out. If she does not react, then the other person has nowhere to go or nothing else to do. She had BIG plans for her bubble.

Session 3 – Thought Training and Development

After checking on Linda's progress from the last week, I was very pleased to hear that she no longer saw the comments as an issue. In fact, she had even found the bubble surprisingly useful at home when her younger brothers started fighting and involving her, or when her mother had moaned at her to clean her room. This was amazing, and she couldn't believe how easy it was.

She had arrived as usual with a huge smile on her face. There seemed to be something different about her smile this week. It appeared more genuine. I had received feedback from the deputy head, who sought me out to tell me that her mother was so pleased with the change that she had seen in her little girl already. She was happier, talkative and was spending more time with the family rather than in her room.

As I explained about this week's session, Linda was as attentive as ever. She loved going through the session and repeating both verbally and artistically (although she was much better than me) the content of thought training and development. She thought for a while before telling me that she had a lot of negative thoughts in her head... all the time. It was too big of a jump for Linda to go from ,"I hate being me," to, "I love me," so we explored what would work best for her over the coming week. She was happy to start with, "I am me," which over time became, "I like being me," to, "I love being me," and, "I love me".

She also had plans to become a teacher when she left school. As we explored the steps she had taken already, it became obvious that she had not really done anything about making this a reality. She had done a lot of thinking, which she could now see remains in her head, but she had not put anything in place to make it happen. She had exams coming up in the near future and she had not done her coursework that would reflect on her overall grades. It is what it is and if it is working, then great, but if not, then back to the thought training and development to see what she can do to make it happen. It was not working, so as we looked at the art work (Well, my version of art!), I asked her what she could do to change the outcome that she was currently on track for. She came up with lots of ideas, steps and a way forward that would work for her.

As we came to an end of this session, Linda got up and gave me a great big hug. She said she was really enjoying our time together and was learning so much. Again, she couldn't wait to put it in to practise and her Jepeca homework for this week, which was to repeat to herself, "I am me". I also reminded her that we were halfway through the programme and that my job was to show her 'how to' so she 'can do' and put the changes in place herself. I could not make any of these changes happen; that was her job.

I also repeated to her on a regular basis that we can only change ourselves, we cannot change anyone else, but we can influence their reaction by our reaction! She controls what she lets in and out, and now she also controls the way she thinks.

Session 4 – Emotional Awareness

Linda arrived again this week via my point of contact's office minus make-up, but plus a huge smile. The best thing that had happened to her this week was that she had handed in some coursework, which she was very proud of, and the worst? She couldn't think of anything. She was using the bubble but as I had predicted, the more you use it, the less you need it so she was using it for future gatherings where she thought someone might stare or say something.

This week for Linda was where she addressed the self-harming and eating… or not! She had been so busy putting her bubble in place and remembering her thoughts, that she had realised she had forgotten to not eat. Her self-harming had decreased as well. When I asked about her feelings at the time of self-harming, she said that it felt like a release. The feelings would build up and build up and she would cut herself to release the tense feeling.

As we moved through the emotional awareness session, Linda was processing the information. I could see her thinking, and when she came to her conclusion, she would surface ready for the next instalment. Currently Linda was running on amber or red. This is where she was constantly stressed or angry or annoyed or frustrated, or where she had lost it. As she realised that each feeling has a purpose and would disappear as and when it was acknowledged, she began to disappear in to her thoughts again. This continued until she rose from the ashes... smiling.

Next, how to use the RAG. If she used it, she wouldn't lose it, and that was appealing. Linda had spent much of her time avoiding what her feelings were telling her, so for this session to advise her to listen to them and then act accordingly using those very feelings that she was running from, was interesting and strange.

We went through the RAG and used an example of where she was feeling angry because someone was staring at her. How was she feeling? We agreed angry (well, I asked her and she told me but we did agree on using the isolated and specific feeling for this example). About the situation, again, we had agreed (as above) someone was staring at her. Now, the next part, 'Get your Choices and Options...' easy. Linda came up with about 10 or 11 options that were available to her. From talking to them and asking them if they would like to ask a question to shouting at them and being rude! As we put each of the options in to the reality bubble, she could see that some of them would work out and leave her happy, and others would not work out, instead leaving her sad, lonely and frustrated and in trouble.

As Linda began to understand how the RAG worked, she wanted to put in place another problem. She was occasionally bullied via social media. Wouldn't that make a difference to the result, she asked, eager to find a solution to her apparent wall. So we worked through the RAG until we found her choices and options. She was amazed and delighted at the number of choices she could access. Of course, what she decides to do at the end of the day is totally down to her but she could see that she is the master of her own destiny!

Putting the options in to the reality bubble and thinking of what would happen next allows her the luxury of foresight. The consequences of our actions will provide the future. Following the process that came from a single thought and developed in to reality by past actions or steps beforehand; it makes perfect sense. Linda worked on her options many times. What would happen if she continued to miss meals? What would happen if she continued to self-harm? What would happen if she continued to let the comments and social media in to her bubble? What would happen if she did her coursework? What would happen if she responded to the bullies? What would happen if she took her make-up off? Interestingly, she discovered that if she took her make-up off, she would miss her friendship with my point of contact and her respite when times were tough.

As she used the reality bubble, she had to use her feelings to see if each step would work for. I cannot help her at this point. It is Linda's feelings that will determine whether the idea will work or not, and if it is a good idea or not. If I go and hit her, then I will feel good, until I calm down a bit but then I will be in trouble and will then feel unhappy.

At the end of the session, Linda said she had decided not to go back to her psychologist in London. I advised against this and to keep her appointments but she said she had been attending the psychologist for such a long time and she felt like it was getting her nowhere. She had used the RAG and feels better than she ever remembers so it was her choice to make. I advised her to speak to her mum and put the techniques in place until I saw her for our penultimate session.

Session 5 – Communication

This week, Linda was in a reflective mood. She felt she had come so far is such a short time and her friends were noticing a difference. She no longer had bullying issues and she was able to say and think, and mean, "I like being me," easily. She had not cut herself and she was eating healthily. Her mum thought I was a miracle worker and the teachers were noticing how much happier she was.

This session, we looked at communication and communicating. Linda loved being able to step in to other people's worlds. She was so impressed at being an expert in communicating already. When I asked her how she knew if her mother was in a bad mood, she started to laugh. I listened with interest as she explained that when her mum goes in to a bad mood, she normally turns bright red and starts to shake her fists like a little girl. Of course, it was no laughing matter at the time but, interestingly, it showed that she had observed her body language and tone perfectly!

Speaking about the problem was not a problem for Linda. She was very good at speaking about why she had issues and problems. She had talked for years about her eating and self-harming, and felt very comfortable until she hit the wall! Literally. Then I turned her around and got her to talk about what she could do and how she could reach the outcome that she wanted. This time, she took on a whole different body posture, tone and even used different words. By the end of this week, Linda brought home a feedback form for her mum to fill in.

Session 6 - Final Assessment

Today, Linda came and sat beside me as I filled in the final paperwork from our sessions. I asked her the usual questions, such as what was the best and worst thing that had happened to her. Her reply was as follows: "The best thing was telling my mum how great I feel now before she filled in your feedback form and the worst thing is not seeing you again!" I know, guess who would be using the tissues next!

As you now know, to progress it is important to process, so as I went through the paperwork, I glanced over at Linda and felt like I was in the presence of a very different young lady. She looked more confident, as I could see by her body language.

The following is the feedback that Linda provided on that last session. She enjoyed all of the sessions. They were always funny and she felt that she could tell me anything and not be judged. The Jepeca programme has helped her to filter what people say as she doesn't take it in any more. Her teachers and Mum have noticed a difference and commented on how mature and happy she has been lately. "I felt really down and had no energy. Now I feel more bubbly and more confident in myself. I look at things differently." She found the sessions funny, interesting and helpful, and looked forward to her life and what she has to offer others by just being herself.

A year later, I had the opportunity to revisit and update and monitor the success of the programme. Linda was as bubbly as ever. She was happy and very chatty. She had not been self-harming and was in a relationship. She had done very well in her exams and had progressed onto her A levels. She had many plans for the future and remembered the steps to achieve her goals. Her parents were delighted with her progress and her mum still thinks I am an angel, and I for one am not going to disagree!

Job done...

Two years later, the point of contact completed an update on her progress for a report. She has excelled academically and was supporting other students with similar situations to what she herself originally presented to the Jepeca programme with. She is still a popular girl with a bubbly personality and a great future ahead of her.

"Tom thought others had noticed a difference,
as his teacher said she had seen
an improvement over the weeks.
His mum had mentioned to him
that he was more relaxed and happier at home."

Case Study Number 3

By Julianne Hadden

Reason for referral from point of contact in school

Tom   14 years old   Boy   England

Tom was not a problem at school. His behaviour was 'normal' or no more an issue than the next boy. He had a 'normal' family life, up to this point. He was the youngest of three; two older girls who were married and living locally to him. He had gone below the radar in his early academic life, and looking at his attendance and behavioural records, there was nothing worth mentioning. Of late, his behaviour had started to deteriorate. He was developing an attitude with his teachers and had received several bad behaviour warnings from teachers, even to the point of being sent out of class. He had been receiving additional support in English and maths.

My point of contact phoned home to highlight the issues that had arisen in school over a period of time to be informed that Tom's father was terminally ill. He was going to die. He was given a few months to live and Tom was not coping with the news very well, hence the change in his attitude, behaviour and personality. With this knowledge, Tom would normally be referred to the school counsellor but as there was no space available currently and Tom was getting in to more and more trouble as each day passed, it was suggested that he had access to the Jepeca programme, and that is how I came to meet Tom.

Session 1 – Initial Assessment

Tom came into my room with the weight of the world on his shoulders. He looked so sad and depressed. Talking appeared to be an effort and so I began like I always do by introducing myself and explaining what Jepeca do and how we do it. He sat up as I explained the process, and when I had finished, he asked, "How are you going to help me?" I acknowledged his question with, That is indeed a good question, but we shall be able to answer that at the end of today's session. Does it sound like something that might help?" He said yes, and the rest is history.

I found Tom to be a deep thinker. Someone who thought everything through before answering, and even then the answer was short and to the point. As we progressed through the initial questionnaire on that first session, I couldn't help but feel an admiration for Tom and his current method of dealing with his situation. He had provided his own natural therapy for the sadness that had become his 'normal' home life. His behaviour was reflecting the frustration and helplessness that had become his reality.

His life could, of course, have been better if his dad wasn't ill. He had no idea how to control his emotions, and recently they seemed to be controlling him, understandably. He had no interest in anything and school was just getting in the way of him being able to help his mum. His older sisters were very good to him and often took him to stay at their places, but he wanted to be at home. The trouble was that sometimes his mum would shout at him and this upset him.

By the end of our first session, I told Tom that I would be able to help him but he would have to participate in the next five sessions. I would be able to show him techniques that he would find useful but he would have to put them in place. Before we could begin with the programme, he would have to seriously think about committing to work with me as each session is different, and if he should not turn up, then it would not be possible to catch up. I watched as he thought it all through and then he nodded slowly and said it was worth a shot.

He wanted to behave better at school and at home for his mum. This, along with his coping strategy for the current stress and grief, were our goals. Each session would be tailored so that he could understand how, where and when to put the right technique in place, especially over the coming months.

I noticed as the session progressed that Tom relaxed a little. He did not cry during our session but had a frown on his face the whole time. His shoulders were hunched and he could get very frustrated with himself if he used the wrong word or phrase to describe something. His tone was monotone and he spent most of the session looking at the floor. He was aware that his behaviour at school was unacceptable but he did not know what to do about it, as he felt so frustrated and angry when he was accused of doing something that he felt he had not done.

Tom left at the end of the session by shaking my hand and looked me straight in the eye saying, "Thank you for trying to help me."

Session 2 – Filters

When Tom arrived, he sat in the exact same chair as before, with the exact same pose as before and greeted me with a straight but sad face. I asked him what was the best and worst thing that happened to him since I saw him last. He said that the best was getting out of science as he hated it, and the worst was that his dad was not able to get out of bed at the moment. It was hard watching him as he was never sick, but now he is sick all the time. I did wonder from the language he used if he knew that his dad was dying, or if he knew but was not accepting it. This was never discussed directly with Tom. My point of contact had told me that he knew and I wanted him to access the programme so he could apply it, not talk about something he clearly did not want to discuss.

During this session, I asked Tom to put on the whiteboard people that annoyed him. It did not matter who they were or for what reason, but I wanted him to make a list of people that said things to him directly or through social media (which he informed me that he did not use) that had upset him. He thought long and hard and then mentioned that his spelling was not great. Once I assured him that these sessions were not about spelling but helping him confidently cope with how he filters what is being said to him, he started.

The list was about 11 people long. A few of his family were on the board, including his dad, some teachers and a few peers. I then asked him which one of those did he think we should work with and he picked a teacher for the first person and a peer for the second. I mentioned that he would be able to use the bubble for the entire list but we wouldn't have time to do that today, so we would concentrate on the first two and if he wanted on the next session, we could address some of the others. We could see how he got on.

Tom was pleased with the decision and agreed. As we used the dude (soft play ball which represented the words) to represent the words that his teacher was saying, it became clear that he felt he was being picked on for something he had not done and those that had done it were getting away scot-free. As we went through the technique, he began to realise that what he was doing was not working.   So I put the cycle up to prove a point; not that I need to, but it all helps.

We used the bubble again on his peer that he had identified earlier. This time, he participated a little too eagerly as I requested that he avoid the head and new hair due! For a minute, he forgot where he was and laughed before he quickly regained his composure. I could see from his ability to swap from the other person to himself that he understood the concept. The more we used the dude for hurtful things or annoying words, the more confident he became.

At the end of this session, he asked me why I did not choose his dad to be part of the session I explained that it was him that chooses who we would work with and if he wanted to involve his dad next week, then we could and would. He smiled at me and walked to the door, but not before adding that he was looking forward to seeing me next week.

Session 3 – Thought Training and Development

Tom strode into the room and stood over me for some time before telling me, in a rather high voice, that he had to start counselling this week and he was not happy. I listened to him as he said he just talks about how he feels the whole time and the counsellor never says anything to him. I could tell he was annoyed as he began to pace the room as his voice got louder and louder. There were so many emotions, so I just let him vent.

As he came to a natural halt, his focus came back to me and I patiently waited for him to gather his thoughts before I began. Then I asked him what was the best and worst thing that had happened to him since I saw him last. He started to laugh and told me the best thing was that he used his bubble last week when his mum shouted at him for being on the Xbox. She just calmed down straight away whereas normally they would be arguing for a long time. Amazing. As for the worst thing... well, we already know that. After listening to what he had to say about what was happening, I informed him that the session today would be really beneficial in moving forward.

We explored his normal thoughts and things that he had made happen, including each of the steps that he took the time and energy to make a reality. This was a pleasant experience for him as he reminisced on times he spent with his dad doing things together. As he stood back, he noticed that there was a lot to thinking involved in the simplest of tasks. Not only thinking, but individual steps, which contain many more thoughts of how and what to do to get the task done.

Although it sounds complicated, it really looks simple once on the whiteboard. Tom enjoyed this part of the session and as we explored the negative thoughts that can interfere with his academic ability, he became more talkative. The questions flowed as he expressed an interest in doing better in class and school. Interestingly, he did not mention his father. As we stood back and looked at what we had covered so far, he was surprised at how much thinking goes on behind the scenes.

Then I asked him if there was anything that he would like to make happen in the future. He said he would like to spend more time with his dad, so we put the reality bubble up and talked about the steps that he would need to take to make that happen. He wanted to go to the cinema with him and watch the latest in the series of films that they liked. It was out in May and he was not sure if his dad would be able to go so we worked through what he would need to do to make it happen and what he could do if his dad was not well enough.

We looked at other things he could do with the time he had left with his dad, and what he would or could do to make these things a reality. Tom liked the fact that he was able to do something. He mentioned that he would be able to make many memories by using the thought development process. I mentioned the fact that he could not change anyone, he could only change himself, but he could influence others by his reaction. He had something to think about over the next week. He cleaned the board before he left, humming a tune to himself.

Session 4 – Emotional Awareness

I asked my point of contact how things were with Tom before I started the session. She said he was attending the counselling but was not saying very much. His teacher had mentioned that he was a bit happier in himself. As I waited for Tom to arrive, I thought about what it must be like for him to come to school each day and not know if his dad was going to be alive when he got home. He was doing very well, considering.

Tom was more interactive than he had been in the other sessions but the cloud that hung over him would remain. When asked if he had been putting the filters and thought training and development in place, he smiled and said, "I don't need the bubble now." I wonder why! As for the thought training and development, he found it interesting and talked to his dad about what he was going to do. It sounded like a bonding session, which I could tell from the passion in his voice and the faraway look in his eyes that he cherished.

This week, I asked him about his feelings and emotions. He looked at me and shrugged his shoulders. From here, I let him follow my artistic drawings to explain what it is and how we use it. I asked him where he spends most of his time and he said on amber. He did not like it but he did not know how to get back to green. The examples for this session were mostly based on classroom experiences and situations that had happened with peers. As we explored the rest of the session, he mentioned that he was angry that his dad was sick. His dad was a good man and there were loads of people out there who should be in his place. I listened and when he looked at me for an answer, I offered to use the RAG to explore his options, as what may be right for me may not necessarily be right for him.

He smiled at me as we went through his options and realised that he could use his feelings in many ways. Firstly, to recognise what they are trying to tell him, and secondly, to see if what he is thinking is a good idea. How does it feel? Will it work? What is that feeling and what is it telling you about your choice? Tom had so much choice and so many options. Yes, there are things that you cannot change, but you can choose how you deal with them.

That was it from Tom this week. He was putting in time and effort in class and he was noticing that he could get through some of his more difficult lessons without getting annoyed, and, in turn, the teacher getting annoyed at his annoyance! As I asked him to clean the whiteboard, he paused in front of it once more as if to absorb as much as he could before moving on. I asked him if he wanted a copy of what we had done and he declined.

Sometimes when we work with clients on a flip chart, we offer the clients the work from that session to take home. Some will take it and put in on their bedroom walls, others do not. There is no right or wrong, just our own individual ways, and in Tom's case, his way. Getting Tom to put the programme in to practise in his life requires examples from his situation, it was safe to use the classroom and that is what we did, but he will on reflection put it in to practise with his dad's situation when the time is right... for him.

Session 5 – Communication

Tom was waiting for me in the room this week. He even had my drink of water ready to hand. As I set up, I watched him ready himself for the session. He sat in his usual chair and got the whiteboard ready. Someone was keen! So then I asked how things were... "I had a good week this week. My dad is up and walking, and I am going to do some of the things that I have planned from the list I made after our session." So that was it. Good for him.

Keeping Tom on track this week was a tad difficult as he was so excited to be spending time with his dad, and rightly so. I covered the main part of communication and how we are experts in knowing what people are saying without words. He found it useful to link it back to his classroom situation. Thinking about how things are when he walks in, he is aware if the teacher is in a good mood or not. He can tell who is up to no good and who is working, and so it also works the other way; so too can the teachers tell who is listening and who is not!

Apart from going over the programme to ensure that Tom understood the techniques, the rest of this week was spent listening to an excited boy share some really lovely memories in the making of what him and his dad get up to when nobody is looking. Magic. As he went out the door, he was smiling and I told him I would see him for our last session next week. I don't know if he even heard me!

Session 6 – Final Assessment

This week was an interesting week. Tom had completed the six sessions of the Jepeca programme, and although the cloud was still in situ, he appeared more confident.

On the last session, he felt that the Jepeca programme had helped him with school. He had learned about different things that he didn't know about. Especially the traffic lights and how all the different parts worked, like thinking and filtering. He thought others had noticed a difference, as his teacher said she had seen an improvement over the weeks. His mum had mentioned to him that he was more relaxed and happier at home, although he could not understand why she would think that. I took the opportunity to go through the RAG with him so he could get his choices and options on what he could do to clarify his mum's intention behind the words. Sorted.

He felt better and although he is still attending the counselling, he could not see the point of it. I assured him that the counselling would help him over the coming months, as he would be able to talk to someone impartial at the school. He felt he could concentrate more and if people are being annoying, he could keep them out by using the bubble.

He described his experience as changing, relaxing and exploring. I asked him what the difference between counselling and coaching was, and he thought about it for a while, then said, "In counselling, I talk about my feelings, but in the Jepeca programme, I know what to do with them. It is about getting them out and doing something about them."

A year later, I caught up with Tom; his father had passed away in the summer. I said I was sorry to hear his sad news and asked him how he was, and he surprisingly repeated the question. "How am I? That is a good question?" I am fine, was the answer, after he did a thorough search for an answer that he felt would qualify for how he was feeling at that moment in time.

I asked him if he used the Jepeca programme and he told me that he found the programme was the most helpful when he lost his dad. He was very sad and angry but he recognised that it was OK, and when he looked at the feelings, he did not want to do anything with some of them, and with others, he did so he felt as if he was in control. He had been attending counselling for a while but found it ineffective. He was undergoing a mentoring programme with the head teacher of his school and he did not enjoy it, but he felt that he could not refuse.

I asked the point of contact how he was, and they said he was off the radar and had been for a long time. He was behaving in class and his grades had improved, as did his willingness to try new things. He seemed more settled and happier.

Two years later, Tom has a successful academic career and has not been flagged up for any reason, other than being a nice, polite and productive young man.

"Paula said that she feels happier and more smiley.
Her teachers have commented on how
she appears happier as well,
and she thinks it may be
because of the newfound happiness
that her mum is wanting to spend more time with her."

Case Study Number 4

By Julianne Hadden

Reason for referral from point of contact in school

Paula   14 years old   Girl   England

I was asked to work with Paula because she ran away from school as she was being bullied. She had refused to attend school for weeks and only agreed to return if the school did something about the bullying. The interesting thing was that nobody knew that she was being bullied. She was a popular girl and was doing well academically, so there was no record of her experiencing problems at school.

My point of contact had no record of contact with her and was very surprised when the Head of Year approached him to say there was an issue and it needed to be resolved as her attendance was now also becoming an issue. Although there was little input from the school about the presenting problem, it makes little difference to how I intend to work with Paula. As I am working on her agenda, the end result will be measured by her happiness. It will either work or not, and young people are not backward in coming forward.

I had permission from her mother for Paula to access the programme, although she did mention to the point of contact that it was in fact the bullies that should be put on programmes, not her daughter. My point of contact disagreed, as Paula needed to be able to deal with the bullies confidently.

Session 1 – Initial Assessment

Paula was timid and quiet on the initial assessment, or should I say for the initial part of the initial assessment. I started explaining who I am, what I do and how I was going to achieve this over the coming weeks, and as

I explained, I noticed that she began to relax. The more she relaxed, the more she talked, and the more she talked, the more she relaxed. The cycle was set.

She presented as a well looked after young lady, from a well-to-do background, I thought, as she had a trendy school bag. I know this because as she placed it on display on top of the table, I made a comment on how nice it looked; she smiled and told me, "It's sick," (apparently a word used today to describe something good!). She also had nice new shoes, her hair was dyed a lovely shade of red and perfectly styled. Her nails were also done perfectly, shaped and painted. It was as if she were about to venture on a social outing that required a minimum dress code. She had a lovely tone to her voice, which was controlled for the time being. It appeared as if she were watching everything she was saying, until I had proved myself.

As she was not familiar with the process, I explained how it worked and what each session would help her with. This referral was specifically to do with being bullied. Paula was aware I knew this information as it was mentioned when she walked into the Head of Year's office, where I was waiting for her. When I asked how her life could be better, it opened the floodgates. Everything that had happened to her since she had been in school came tumbling out, and in no particular order. We jumped from her first year in school, to her third year, and back to the second year randomly.

Each year had a reoccurring theme. It would start with how someone said this and the others laughed, and then I tried to say something back (big mistake) and they said something else. Sometimes it would involve throwing stuff or pushing. Sometimes it could even go as far as being set upon outside of school with physical abuse; thankfully, in this case, it had not. None of the above is pleasant. None of the above is right. None of the above is or should be accepted as the norm, and none of the above can be ignored!

Paula would react to each and every taunt. It was this reaction that amused the bullies. She had, in fact, a choice of reactions but chose to react in the same way every time. This is when I brought the Jepeca Cycle in to the session and she saw that the way she was dealing with it was not working. Something had to change and it was within her power to make that change a reality by using the techniques we would work on over the following weeks.

The interesting thing about bullying is that there is no rhyme or reason to it. Someone one day says or does something and your reaction is what changes everything. If you react one way, then it means this will happen, but if you react another way, then something else will happen. For example, one client I worked with (let us call him A) was bullied regularly on the way home on the bus for listening to music on his iPod with his earphones. As a result, his reaction was to turn it down and pretend that he did not hear them. Of course, they knew that he had heard them because he reacted, and this was the catalyst for many months of bullying – until he did the Jepeca programme.

The words used never matter, they really don't. This may seem unbelievable, but think about it. If someone were talking to you or at you in a different language, it would be the tone and body language that would indicate if it is harmless or harmful. Bullying still occurs with people who do not understand the language, and very successful bullying, I many add. In fact, it was client A's reaction that caused the amusement that led to many months of torture, sadness and loneliness. How it is said never matters either. Remember, it is how you react that will determine how your next encounter unfolds. This is, after all, how you influence others. Your reaction will have a part in the outcome of a situation, but it is changeable, and so too is the outcome.

Another client was in a very desperate state because she was being called a 'man'. I thought there was maybe more to it but constant, repetitive, snide, sneaky jibes in the corridor, outside school and online had left her in a sad, lonely and very desperate place. What may seem trivial to the majority can seem overwhelming to one specific person, and that is important, because if it is a problem for one person, it is a problem. The commonest advice given in such cases of bullying is to ignore it! How? That is what clients have being trying to do, unsuccessfully. That is usually why they have sought you out and asked for help; you are someone they think may be able to do something. Ignoring it is not an option. They need to feel in control and empowered.

In fact, it was a comment that caused a reaction for client A. How it is said never matters. The experts we naturally are at reading reactions via body language, allow us to clock that split second when you have 'got to' someone. With a little more probing and testing of how much we have 'got to' them by judging their reactions to other bullying behaviour, will determine what will happens next.

Now back to Paula's situation. I think it is important to mention that Paula had friends. She had many good friends who were supporting her throughout the bullying. Her family was very supportive, so much so that her mother was going to keep her at home until all of the bullies were excluded, or at least dealt with. They had even thought of moving schools. My concern with moving schools would be that the necessary skills to deal with bullies would not be learned, and should the client encounter this issue again, they will react in exactly the same way. It is an essential life skill that enables the individual to confidently deal with life's challenges and changes, as and when necessary.

After I explained the layout of the following sessions, she sat and thought for a bit. She couldn't believe that next week, we would be working on her issue, and she would have something to take away and use immediately. In fact, she was so excited she asked if we could start today but I advised against it. First, I needed to get the bigger picture. I needed to step in to her world for a brief moment in time and look at things from her perspective, hear how she was hearing the things that were being said to her, and get her thoughts and feelings on her life in general. After all, it is her agenda I am working on.

Previous experiences also tells me that, although it may sound like a great idea to provide all of the information and techniques at once, the client is NOT able to process them and when precious processing time is lost, so too is the window of opportunity to empower them. I want this to work for every client. I want them to be happy with being them, in control of their life's journey and productive with whatever they put their minds too. Slowly, slowly catchy monkey, and I had time on my side, as well as patience :)

The rest of the initial assessment and initial questionnaire appeared to go smoothly. There were no issues anywhere else, apart from the bullying. As Paula got up to leave, she had a huge smile on her face. She asked me if I could really help her and I said, "YES, 100%. It is my job. I can show you 'how to' use the Jepeca programme so you 'can do' when you need it. I cannot use it for you, that is your job." She appeared very excited and left my room smiling.

Session 2 - Filters

Paula was waiting for me outside the room as I arrived for this week's session. As I unlocked the door, I noticed there were some students hanging around, watching her from a safe distance. Walking into the room, I noticed that she gave a small friendly wave to the watchers as if to say, "It's OK now, I am safe." I do admire the young people of today. They can form some amazing bonds and friendships at school. Of course, this all changes over time, but the learning therein is amazing.

Checking with Paula how her week went, I discovered that she was still being taunted in the corridors, hence the bodyguards outside in the corridor! It had been a difficult week as she had missed so much school and catching up with the curriculum was no easy task, but she appeared determined and focused. The best thing that happened to her was that she got tickets to see her favourite band with her older sister. The worst was the bullying that she had mentioned earlier. It was all starting to build up again and the thought of doing this session had kept her going.

Right then, let's get started. I first asked her to write the names of the people on the whiteboard that she felt were bullying her. Then when she had completed that, I asked her to circle the main ones and then the person she felt was the ringleader. Next, I asked her to share some typical bullying situations that really frustrated her. Scene set...

This session was the one Paula had been waiting for. She had no idea what was about to happen and her nerves really helped set the scene. She was nervous and giggly, and her bubble was in perfect working order. The fact that she always had a bubble shocked her, and she loved that it would be the main source of protection from this day forth.

Her way of personalising it was really interesting and fun; not only did she put a colour on the bubble, which was baby pink with bright purple stripes, but it also had a texture of silk-like metal so it could give maximum protection. I told her she could always change it later if she wanted. Nothing was set in stone, to which she replied that she now wanted to change the texture to stones of different colours. She also furnished it, decorated it and designed it to her specification. Go, Paula! :)

When it came to actually using the bubble, Paula found it difficult to step in to the bully's shoes. This is an important part of the exercise and I told her that she would understand the importance of it at the end. It took a lot of courage to see how her bully saw her and to hear herself say the hurtful things that he had been saying to her, but it is an important step so she decided to give it a go. It did not take long for the role play to be a brief glimpse of what Paula felt was happening to her on a daily basis. She was surprised at how powerful and happy the bully felt when she was role playing being him as he was being nasty to me (who was role playing her) without my bubble.

Perfect.

The next part was where I was being Paula with my wonderful new bubble with its all-singing, all-dancing add-ons! Paula got ready to play the bully and it began again. She was doing her best to get me to react but it was useless. I, of course, have an excellent bubble that has weathered many storms, successfully. After a very short time, Paula could see that it was pointless and called a halt to the whole exercise.

I did not even get to ask her what she thought, as she launched in to rapid description of how awful it felt being the bully this time. It made perfect sense to her now and she felt really stupid being the bully shouting at me but getting no reaction. Bingo. The penny drops. Then I ask her how does she think it looks for the other young people around to see the bully shouting at her and not getting a reaction. She thought for a second and replied, "He would feel like I did for all those years." He will learn that you are not going to give him the reaction that you normally did. Things have changed and there is a new sheriff in town. Watch this space.

As we finished up the second session, I informed her that it would be wise to visualise the bubble every night for the next week, because the more you use it, the less you need it. She could change it as much as she wanted, or leave it as it is; it is her choice and her bubble. Nobody else knows she has a bubble or what she does with it. It's up to her if she wants to share that information. She will never be without her bubble again. Happy bubble time. She left the room looking forward to seeing her bullies, would you believe it!

Session 3 – Thought Training and Development

I was so looking forward to working with Paula again to hear about her experiences with using the bubble. When I got to the room, she was, as had become a ritual, waiting outside for me with a huge grin on her face. I took that as a sign that it worked! As I unlocked the door, I noticed there were no bodyguards around – another good sign. Walking into the room, I barely had time to take my coat off or close the door before she began to tell me of her last week's adventures.

After school as she went for the bus, she had to walk past the main bully, the one which she had pretended to be during our session. Now was the moment of truth. She said her heart was pounding and she felt nervous, but confident that it would work. In fact, she likened it so something exciting like going on a theme park ride! She was aware of what was going to happen, but also what she was going to do. Bubble up, ready for use...

As she walked past, he started to shout the usual names, making fun of her and her posh bag, and the way she spoke. Paula was bouncing those comments in all directions, including right back at him. She kept her focus on where she was going and talked to her friends (bodyguards) as if nothing had happened. Her friends were surprised that she was going to let him talk to her like that and asked her if she was going to do anything about it, to which she replied, "I am," and smiled sweetly as she carried on the conversation. Everyone was shocked. This was a totally new reaction and it influenced everyone around her in such a positive way.

Her bully was shocked and upped his game by getting very personal and calling her family all sorts... No reaction.

Change of tactics on the bully's part, he tried to get other people involved to tease her and laugh at her, but it all turned around and backfired.

What actually happened, she explained, was that those boys and girls that had been bullying, laughing and making fun of her over the years told him to stop being an idiot. They walked over to Paula and started talking to her, and she could not stop smiling. Her friends were in shock, and that was the end to her bullying in secondary school.

Paula did practise the bubble at night, as I had advised, and found it really helpful. She would recall memories of past experiences at times and put the bubble in place to protect herself; this, she mentioned, made her feel happy. She also used it to visualise in the morning before she got out of bed so that should anyone say anything to her, she would automatically put the bubble in place and feel safe and secure. It showed in her confidence and the excited voice as she told of her victory.

I explained to Paula that the bully will have some issues as well, so she had to be careful not to turn the tables and become the bully. Whatever was going on at home or in school for him resulted in his behaviour. By looking at the Jepeca Cycle, we could see it was not working, but was the only way he knew of dealing with things for the minute. Hopefully, he would be lucky enough to access our programme, but funding in schools does not cater for everybody. There is specific funding available for some, while others go without as they do not qualify. It is a great shame as they need the help just as much, but in this case the school's hands were tied, and all because he was not receiving free school meals.

This got Paula thinking, and much as she enjoyed her victory, she also thought that things were not easy at home for her bully so she was not going to make things more complicated.

Before I moved on to the session we were doing this week, I asked her if anything bad had happened this week and, not surprisingly, she said no; she was very happy.

This session went as planned and Paula found it very interesting for her forthcoming exams. She was a very good student who always handed in her homework and was intending to go on to further education. Because of the chunk of school she missed due to running away, she was eager to attend catch-up sessions and she found this thought training and development was putting her in control of what she was going to do. She also mentioned that she was going on holiday to Florida this year and had put a lot of research in to the different parks. She began to see a pattern emerge that not only was she getting up and doing something about achieving things, but she put a lot of research in to everything she did. From getting a new mobile phone, to her holiday activities, to where sold the CD she wanted, to her homework. It all fitted together nicely.

Session 4 – Emotional Awareness

By this week, the bullying was a thing of the past. There were no bodyguards waiting outside and Paula was back on track, albeit with a large amount of schoolwork to catch up on, which she did not complain about. She used her family experiences for this week and it emerged that there is a bit of tension at home sometimes as her older brother expected her to wait on him hand and foot when her mum was not around.

As we went through the traffic lights, Paula told me that she used to be on amber all the time, but as the bullying had stopped she was on green at school but amber at home when her mum was at work. We worked through her different scenarios using her experiences and memories to enable her to understand how the techniques would work for her.

I asked her to write on the board the names of those that were causing her to go up to amber. There was just her brother and her mum sometimes. For this, we went through each situation and used the RAG to examine her options. Then she made her choices of what she thought would work and put each in to the reality bubble of thought training and development, and we discussed the steps that she would have taken to make it a reality and where that would lead.

Interestingly, bullying was not mentioned but if it had been mentioned again, as occasionally we have clients who say that the comments have seeped through the bubble, this is where we would explore what would happen next. You always have a choice and option available to you, ALWAYS. You can do something, or you can do nothing. If you do nothing, then nothing will change. If this makes you happy, calm or relaxed, then you are going in the right direction. Paula got the idea very quickly. If the bullying is physical, then that is assault and the school, your parents or the police will take that very seriously.

We worked through some of the cycles that Paula noticed at home and used the RAG and thought training and development to work out a solution that she thought might work. Nothing is set in stone so if she wanted to change it at any time, then she had the ability and know-how to do so.

Session 5 – Communication

This week, Paula was waiting outside with her friends, who she wanted to introduce. As I unlocked the door, she arranged to meet them after school in the usual place, and each and every one of them said goodbye to both Paula and I. It was nice to see normality being restored to her life and academic career. This girl had big plans, and I am looking forward to hearing about them in the future. Things could have been so different!

We spent this week working on her family again. There were the normal teenage niggles that can so easily take over the family's time together. Moaning, groaning, tantrums, "Why me? It is always me," "I hate you," and all sort of things. Paula knew she did this sometimes but she also knew it was a cycle that did not work for her so she was more than happy to explore options or ways of communicating that would work.

Paula was also a keen social butterfly. She used many well-known social media sites and this had increased since the bullying stopped, but the tension and anger at home had increased as her flittering from site to site increased! Interestingly, another cycle emerging but one that she recognised straight away. Looking at the way in which she communicates, she realised that she needs to verbally spend time with her family in order for relations to develop in a positive way. That had not been happening and they were missing her. So we developed a plan that she could put in place at home by using her RAG to get her choices and options, her traffic lights to get if it was the way forward specifically for her, and her reality bubble to explore the steps that would need to be in place to make it happen.

Paula was still working on the whiteboard as I did my notes, and by the end of our session, she had a few suggestions that she was going to approach her older brother with, as well as a suggestion for her mum on how they could spend time together. Looking back at where Paula started, she had come a long way. She had grown in confidence and self-esteem, and I met her Head of Year before I left who informed me that she was a lot happier. She had nearly caught up with the work she had missed, and as she was back on track, they had high hopes for her academic future.

In case I have not said it before, I love my job. The clients I work with make it all possible, and in the short time I spend with them, they are so receptive and desperate to change the way things are in their life but they simply do not know how. I know for the other coaches that this is true also for them. I even hear coaches singing on voicemail about the results they are getting (you know it is true, Katie!). The changes the Jepeca programme is making to the lives of young people is amazing. Our clients are looking for a way to move forward, a way of being happy, just being who they already are, a way of being in control of their lives and the direction they are going in and a way of being productive at home and with their time.

Session 6 - Final Assessment

The final assessment comes around all too quickly. I love this week for many reasons. The client gets to explore the shift that has occurred in the last few weeks, the school gets the opportunity to reflect on progress, the parents get a chance to input their observations and I, as the coach, get to calibrate the client to provide the evidence that I was speaking about earlier! It's all good! :)

In Paula's case, her Head of Year was pleased that she was back in school and back on track with her studies. Her mum was happy that she was happy, and that just left Paula to explore her recent six-week trip through the Jepeca programme.

Paula was smiling as she found a comfortable place to sit in anticipation of what was to happen. I asked as usual, "What was the best and worst thing that happened to you since I saw you last?" question and she informed me that there was nothing bad but that she was excited about going out with her friends at the weekend.

As we progressed through the paperwork and questionnaire, I was surprised that there was no mention of bullying! Very surprised, as it was, after all, the reason for her absence from school and the reason why she had so much homework! I wanted the evaluation to be as accurate as possible and so from her perspective, I decided not to mention it – just yet...

Moving on, she said that she felt she could be really open and honest and talk freely during the sessions. She loved the bubble and found it really useful, although she mentioned that she did not need to use it as much lately!

When asked if it had helped with any issues, I expected her to mention the bullying, but again, there was no mention. I couldn't believe it. It had helped with family issues, things at home. She thought about it and said that as she looked back, she could see that she gets on much better with her family, especially her brother and her mum. Interestingly, she mentioned that it helped with nightmares as well. Apparently she woke in the middle of the night from a nightmare where she thought someone was trying to get into her room, and she immediately used her bubble, traffic lights, RAG, then thought training and development to return to a calm relaxed state. Note to self – works with nightmares.

Paula said that she feels happier and more smiley. Her teachers have commented on how she appears happier as well, and she thinks it may be because of the newfound happiness that her mum is wanting to spend more time with her. She mentioned that she believes in herself a lot more and this was down to the thought training and development technique. She has used this technique to help her in her exams as well. Several times, she was going to give up on her test papers but after she sat and thought it through, she decided that it would not serve a purpose to quit and she remembered what I had said: "If you are doing your best, then you are being your best." She was very pleased with herself, and rightly so! :)

Moving on with the feedback form, I asked Paula what the biggest difference she had noticed now to how she was before she began the Jepeca programme, and for a moment I lost her. She went inside, put her head down, and was very still and quiet. Right, I thought to myself, now I shall hear about the bullying. Getting ready to write her response, I noticed a slight smile cross her face before she began to speak. The biggest difference was that she talks to her family more now and that they are a lot closer which makes her feel happier. Yes, she repeated, I am so much happier now. Still nothing about the bullying! Strange.

The three words she used to describe her experience were helpful as in being happier and having a closer family, understanding as in she understands things a lot more now, and informative as in she now knows what to do if she wants to change something.

Was there anything that could improve the sessions? Long pause....no.

OK, that was the end of our session, questionnaire and programme. But I had to ask her about the bullying. After all, that was the reason for her referral in the first place! I would need to make reference to this in the final report to the point of contact. As it was, the point of contact only recently mentioned that he could think of several students that would benefit from being able to deal with teachers, family and peers who offer unhelpful, hurtful and nasty comments. He expressed an interest in the final report and Paula's turning point...

As I went through the final part of the session and explained that no matter what happened throughout her life, she would always be able to return to the Jepeca programme to help her find her own answer or solution to the presenting challenge, she nodded enthusiastically. I asked her if she had any questions and she asked if she would ever see me again. This part of the session is sad in some ways, but so exciting in others. The client is in a very different place. They are empowered to make the changes they want to see in their lives. Our job is done; we have shown the 'how to' so they 'can do'.

I looked at Paula and said, "What happened to the bullying? How come you did not mentioned it in the feedback?" She simply turned to me and said, "But that was a long time ago. I have not been bullied for ages." It made perfect sense, to her, and when I thought about it, to me as well.

This is something we see regularly in schools and was displayed perfectly by Paula. When an issue is no longer an issue, it simply ceases to exist. If I want them to think or talk about it, I have to draw their attention to that particular problem and get the person to access that memory for what was, as currently it is not an issue! Often in conferences or meetings, I ask professionals about young people we have previously worked with, that were so difficult and had many issues or concerns that they took up a lot of resources and time. After the Jepeca programme, they are no longer a problem, and so the next issue a young person flags up, until the original problem fades into the background. They usually have a think and then tell me that they are accessing the curriculum and are no longer an issue, but they have huge issues and concerns with Tom and Dick and Harry, or Tammy, Doris and Harriet. For Paula, it was exactly the same. As her bullying was no longer an issue, it simply did not exist. The party at the weekend was her focus now, not her exams, the bullying or her fear of meeting one of her bullies outside of school. And even if it were an issue, Paula would know what to do to make the change happen.

I checked on Paula's progress six months later with my point of contact. She is no longer flagging up, and she is no longer an issue or concern to the school. When he asked for feedback from other teachers, they said that she was a delight, always on time with her equipment ready and an attitude to match.

The Jepeca programme is fast, effective and measurable. Paula had transferred the skills, tools and techniques she had learned during our sessions in to her academic life, her social life and her home life. The original referral was for bullying but the referral reason does not really matter. What matters is how she thinks, feels and filters what is going on around her. She is now happy, in control and productive.

"Colin described the programme as fun, enjoyable, amazing and life-changing."

Case Study Number 5

By Julianne Hadden

Reason for referral from point of contact in school

Colin   11 years old   Boy   England

Colin was referred for low confidence and low self-esteem. His behaviour in class was an issue and he had, as a result, spent many breaks outside the head teacher's office. The result of this was that he would have to stay in at break and he would always argue his case that it was not his fault but that of the other children, who started it first. The more frustrated he became, the more verbal displeasure for the injustice of his treatment, and so the cycle continued, but always with Colin missing breaks!

He was a big boy for his age, and as a result, was often challenged on the playground. He preferred to spend his time playing with the girls at break and during PE. My point of contact was desperate as his teacher tended to be overgenerous with her punishment and observations of his flaws! This, of course, did not help with his self-esteem, and so the cycle continued.

My point of contact mentioned there may be issues for Colin with regard to his sexuality in time to come, and their fear was that with his current state of mind and appearance, he may not cope well in the future.

Session 1 – Initial Assessment

Colin entered the room as if he were a mouse caught in an elephant's body. Strange image, I suppose, but he appeared very quiet and timid, and tripped up on his scarf as he made his way to the chair. This caused his bag to open and all of its contents to spill onto the floor. As he began to reassemble his belongings, he kept saying sorry. When he finished, he looked at the seating options and picked a chair that was near the door and also the furthest away from me. I gave him time to settle before I spoke. He avoided eye contact and picked his fingers.

I started by telling him about me, what I do, how I do it and what each session involves, including what the sessions can help with. His interest picked up as he leaned in a little bit closer. I continued with explaining that in today's session, we would need to cover paperwork, and as there was much to do, I would appreciate his help in working out what exactly he needed to get from the Jepeca programme. He had by now pulled his chair right in to the table and relaxed his shoulders. I noticed he was nodding his head but still picking his fingers so I offered my alternative – would he prefer to draw, colour, doodle, make something with the putty-like substance I usually had for sticking things on the wall, or did he have something else he could think of doing whilst listening? Choices, choices... This he loved and looked me in the eye for the first time.

I notice that there are many children (and adults, including myself) who prefer to keep their hands busy whilst listening to what is happening around them. I always encourage my clients to find a way that will be comfortable for them whilst I go through the programme. It does not mean that they are not listening. It does not mean that they are being disrespectful. It allows them the ability to occupy their hands whilst their brains can engage comfortably at a pace that suits them. I also find that it enables them to relax and frees their tongue! True. Whilst they are distracted with 'doing,' they process what is being said and add in when and where they feel is necessary. It works beautifully.

Colin decided on the 'putty stuff', as he called it, for today, anyway. He started rolling, and I started asking. As I went through the initial assessment, I noticed that he had difficulty in agreeing to voice his opinion if he disagreed with something. He mentioned that if he did this at home, he would get in to trouble so I explained that I needed him to not only understand what I was going to tell him, but for him to be able to use it and if he did not agree, then he would not use it and so it may not work. I watched him struggle with this for a few minutes. Eventually he said, "OK, I will tell you but can I remind you that you asked me too?" Perfect, and so we moved on to the next part.

Behaviour was an interesting topic. Colin felt he was not the problem but was just reacting how everyone expected him too. He had developed a reputation and said that was what people expected. He did not want to misbehave, but when others did, they seemed to get away with it. He felt that his teacher did not like him, and so what was the point of being good for her and making her life easy? As he said, "If I misbehave long enough, maybe she will leave the school!" All in all, he knew what he was doing was not working and was grateful to get the opportunity to work on it.

He felt his self-esteem was very low and did not know what to do about it. His confidence was OK but could be better, or at least pointed in the direction. His behaviour, both at school, as mentioned above, and at home, was an issue. He was always fighting with his sister and as she was younger, he was blamed for causing the fight. Again, he thought it unfair but did not know how to change it, as she was pretty annoying at times.

Colin had scars on his body for where cysts had bust. He found these embarrassing. Nobody in the school knew about these cysts, but many knew about the scars. As I listened, I heard how the scars were just as painful as the cysts, but in a different way. Colin's teacher had mentioned that physical education (PE, or games) were difficult, as Colin would mess about and refuse to get changed. By the time he had changed, he had disrupted the lesson so much, many of the boys were annoyed with him and there could be angry words exchanged. Now it all made sense.

I explained to Colin that I would have to tell my point of contact about the cysts as it also explained why on occasion during playtimes that he would get very angry with people who bumped in to him accidentally. They had, of course, bumped in to one of the cysts and this is what hurt Colin, but as nobody knew about them, it was assumed that Colin was being Colin, attention-seeking and overreacting. He had never thought of it like that and was very supportive of sharing the news.

I discovered through the questionnaire that Colin was not happy and did not feel safe. He had a feeling that someone was going to take his mother away. His father had been in prison and Colin was watching the whole situation unfold as the police came and took him away. The feeling that the same thing would happen to his mother could be overwhelming at times.

Home life was what it was. By that, I mean that Colin was used to his home circumstances and whatever he was to tell me would not make any difference to the way it was, as many other professionals knew as well. I knew this, as did he. The bigger picture is necessary to understand and ensure that the agenda remains with the client. This is their story, their reality, and as Jepeca coaches, we are interested to hear what they have to say.

Colin thought that if he could believe in himself, then it would make a difference to what he would do and could do in the future. He enjoyed singing and using computers, as well as art, but hated football and, as he put it, any boy's games.

The sad thing is Tom hated being him. When asked, he said if he could be anyone else, it had to be better than being him. He described himself as, "Nothing," "I am just a person," and, "UGLY". He really wanted to change the way he looked and get rid of the scars. But as that was not possible, there was no hope.

WRONG!

I went through the forms at the end of the session and told Colin that I could help him. I would show him 'how to', so he 'can do'. He looked at me and I asked him if he believed me, to which he replied, "YES." Now all that was left was to set the goals he wanted us to work on. Confidence, self-esteem and behaviour. He smiled for the first time and disappeared off in to his mind. When he came back, he looked at me and said, "Thank you, thank you for helping me."

I had a word with his teacher on the way out and she agreed to give him the space he needed to put his new techniques in place over the next few weeks. I usually find the teachers are very helpful and want all children to benefit from their time in school. Mind you, saying that, I have come across a couple who seem to have forgotten why they entered the teaching profession, but I am glad to say they are few and far between. They have a large class of students, and identifying and meeting the needs of every single young person is nearly impossible. The majority do an amazing job and have the patience of a saint.

People do not enter the teaching or nursing profession to become rich. Most are dedicated individuals who have a desire to help mould and shape the minds of the future, and/or make a difference. Teachers too have lives and roads to travel. Our mission at Jepeca is to enhance their teaching experience so that they can fulfil their mission. We are all working together for a common goal: to help young people reach their potential, to the best of their ability whilst enjoying the experience, and to be happy, in control and productive.

Session 2 – Filters

Colin was still quiet as he came to the session this week. He was sporting a very colourful, long and flowing scarf. He sat a little closer to me this week, and as I started the session, I asked him what was the best thing that happened to him since I saw him last.

"Nothing."

"OK then, what was the worst thing that has happened to you since I saw you last?"

"I got two more cysts."

"OK. Are you OK to do the session today?"

"I have been waiting all week," he replied, and so we began.

Because Colin was a big boy, and by that I mean that he was often mistaken for a 14 or 15-year-old, he would get called names. His sense of fashion was also very individual, and this drew some glances and rude, unnecessary comments at times. This session would benefit him greatly.

As he would be transferring to secondary school during the year, there was a concern that he may encounter the harshness that teenage years can often lend themselves too!

As I explained what would happen in this session, Colin listened with great interest. He was busying his hands with the putty stuff and throwing out the odd comment that was valid and asking interesting questions. Right now, I needed some examples to work in to the technique so he could understand and use them at his leisure. He thought that his sister would be a good start as she was so very irritating and he constantly got in to trouble with his mum. I couldn't agree more and commended him on his tolerance of her to date. This amused him and he chuckled before continuing to tell me that nobody ever said anything nice to him.

Colin found it fun to participate in the bubble; he loved personalising it and laughed his way through testing it. On reflection, I wondered when was the last time he laughed so hard. He relaxed during our session and even sat closer to see what I was writing in the notes. He understood how it worked and thought it would be perfect for using on his younger sister. He also wanted to practise using it on some of the boys who could be rough in school. I told him the bubble would work for the name calling but if it started to get physical, then he would have to tell someone and we would work on that in week four.

A lot of Colin's issues with his sister and friends were because one person wanted the other to do something and they did not want to do it. Sound familiar? As adults, falling out of favour with other adults, or come to think of it, young adults in the making, bears a striking similarity. One person asks, insists or thinks that the other should do things their way. No compromise, no checking if it would work for the other person, just this is how it will be done! Think about it? The other person does not want to, and so a cycle begins. For some people, the penny never drops. For others, reading this, hopefully, those cogs will start turning in a direction of realisation. But then there are the few who will get caught in the cycle time and time again, constantly falling out with people, taking one minute, not the next, it is always someone else's fault. If you are constantly falling out with people, ask yourself, "Am I being selfish by expecting people to do it my way or demanding of their time? Am I letting them be themselves?" You may be surprised! Believe it. We are born with everything we will ever need to get through this life – no money, no mobile phones and no clothes, and NO person telling you what to do, apart from that little voice in your head. Live and let live.

Session 2 - Thought Training and Development

I looked forward to working this session with Colin from week one. I knew this would help him with his confidence and self-esteem issues, but also his dislike for being himself. He had many issues that were linked back to the way he thought about himself and this impacted on his actions just as much as his feelings. It was important to ensure that he understood this session.

The best thing that happened to him this week was using his bubble successfully on his sister. It, as predicted, drove her mad and then she soon realised that she would have to talk to Colin nicely if she wanted a reply. It is a very quick learning process with short, sharp results not to be taken lightly. Colin enjoyed the new power he had mastered immediately and told me it was even working when he walked home. I had not known but he usually walks home after school and some older boys were making fun of his scarves, but now he told me couldn't hear them and wore what he wanted and he felt happier doing so.

Working through thought training and development, Colin was shocked at how many thoughts we have a day. He loved learning about computers and wanted to put the reality bubble in to practise straight away. I tried to understand what he was talking about, but as my husband could tell you, technology and me don't mix. I love using it and that is where it ends. Colin loved explaining his computer stuff and I loved listening.

As we moved on to the next part of how he uses his thoughts to make the negative thoughts real as well, he became quiet again. I firstly explained how it worked and then did the usual examples of, "I can't," and, "I am stupid". Colin listened with interest, nodding enthusiastically. Then

I asked him what other examples he could think of that he repeats to himself on a regular basis. The list was endless and each one we worked through and flipped it over to a positive. As I got Colin to step back and see what he could notice, he said that he could not believe how many negative thoughts he had and how often. Perfect.

One thought I will share with you from Colin's negative collection was his thought that he was ugly. This, for many reasons, including his cysts and the fact that all of his relations seemed to pay compliments to his sister, never to him, reinforced the fact that he must indeed be ugly. The jump for Colin to go from being 'ugly' to, "I love me," was too painful and difficult so we looked at what he could and would be happy to say. For a start, it was, "I am me," with a view to moving on to, "I like being me," to "I love being me," to "I love me". He happily said he would put that in to place this week, so every time he thought to himself, "I am ugly," he would say STOP in his head and say, "I am me," instead. This, he said, would be good when it was time to get read for P.E.

As I discussed the coming week with Colin, I repeated that he could use the bubble as needed for past, present and future situations, circumstances and situations. He could now also think his way (if he wanted) out of, or in to, better ones. He loved it, and when we finished this session, he stood up, came over as I was writing, and gave me a huge hug. So not expected, but much appreciated.

Session 4 – Emotional Awareness

Colin had a great week, both at school and at home. I met with his teacher and discussed his situation. She said that she could see an improvement and was giving him the space we had discussed. It was making a difference and she had altered some of the student seating to incorporate this newfound confidence.

Colin had an incident at school where someone bumped in to him and burst one of his cysts. Thankfully, as the school were aware, they kept an eye on it ,and although he was upset and his mother was informed, he decided he wanted to stay in school. He told me later that he was surprised at how understanding the school were as he had thought they would not want him in school with such horrible things. Couldn't be further from the truth.

As we worked on this session, Colin got a little upset. He realised that it was OK to be sad that his dad was not at home. It was OK to be angry with his sister for making fun of his skin. It was OK to be annoyed with the boys in school for making fun of him for not wanting to play football. There is no right or wrong; there is only his way and my way. If it works, then great! If not, then we find another way, but something will work. If he gives up looking, then he will never find it.

Looking at the whiteboard, Tom could see that he spent most of his time on amber and red. He wanted to get down to green and when I explained the RAG, he spent ages going through different choices and options available to him. He loved it.

"I could hit those boys, I could shout at them, I could kick them but let's put that in to the reality bubble."

"Now, will that work out for you?"

"No."

"OK, go again."

"I could tell the teacher. I'll put it in the reality bubble."

"Will that work?"

"It might do. I could tell my mum."

"Will that work?"

"No. Next, I could run away. I'll put it in the reality bubble."

145

"Will that work?"

"No." And so it continued until he found what would work for him, and what he thought would work, and what he had been doing but it did not work.

Colin was also used to hearing about his anger problem from his relations. "I don't like it when we all get together because they start to side with my mum and tell me I am like my dad and will end up in prison, and it really makes me angry."

"I am not surprised, that would make me angry as well. So what are you going to do about the next family gathering? You know, it will probably come around to it again, so what are you going to do? If you do nothing, nothing will change, so do something." This is the control I mentioned, and this is breaking the cycle, or taking the bull by the horns.

So we worked through his next family gathering. He used the RAG to get his choices and options. We checked with the traffic lights to see if there were any other feelings that needed to be recognised, and then put his options in to the reality bubble, and by using his traffic lights again, we decided if the choice he made would work for him or not. Did it get him back to green? Easy peasy! :)

Session 5 – Communication

So this was our penultimate week. Colin was sad that he would not see me again. He said he liked the sessions and enjoyed having his opinion listened to. Interesting and fair comment, as not many people listen today. How many people actually listen or take the time to ask questions about you and your interests or day? Sad, but true; its all, "Me me me!" these days.

This leads on nicely to communication, as Colin was communicating internally long before he was communicating externally. He was a master at body language, and after I explained how it all works, he listened with great interest. During the past few weeks, we had looked at how he could control the communication internally by listening to the signals for his feelings and training or developing his thoughts as he saw fit. Now how could he tell what was going on outside him or with others?

The clues are all around us. Our tone, body language and words are unconscious signals to others and received immediately. From here, we decide what will happen next or how we are going to react. Colin's teacher had mentioned that he had been working out a maths problem the other day and when someone asked him if he needed help, he shouted at them. On further exploration, Colin could see that it was not the best response and what he wanted to do was work it out himself but it did not come out like that. He also thought that he would look stupid, and when we went back to the traffic light and RAG and reality bubble, he found a better way of doing things.

Session 6 – Final Assessment

This week, Colin was sitting beside me as we completed the paperwork. I explained what we were going to do this week and asked him how things had gone for him the past week. He said, "Do you mean what was the best and worst thing that has happened to me?" I thought, clever boy! He said that he didn't have anything bad but he was going to his friend's house after school.

Going over the paperwork, Colin said that his whole life had changed. He felt so different. I mentioned that he looked different as well, as he looked me in the eye with a smile. His cysts had improved for the minute and he felt confident that when they returned, he would have support at the school. He felt like he was a special person and he liked being him. He had not quite got to, "I love me," but he was able to say and believe that he liked being him.

The changes span right across Colin's life. As his confidence and happiness grew, so too did his world. He described himself as 'happy', 'a nice person' and 'fun'. So different to his initial assessment!

Colin had attended counselling twice before and had not found it useful. He was dubious about the Jepeca programme and his commitment had paid off. He told me he found the bubble, thought training and development, together with the RAG, most useful. He used them every day and was beginning to discover, as I had once told him, that the more he used them, the less he would need them.

Interestingly, he told me something that he had not mentioned before, which allowed me a glimpse in to the life that must have been before he participated in the Jepeca programme. He said that he could now take pictures of himself. Before if he had to have a picture taken, which he hated, he used to take pictures and edit them. Now he said that he could have a picture taken without editing them. Can you imagine what that must have been like? A boy of 11 years old editing his own image because it was not good enough!

He said he was much happier now. He feels much better. His biggest difference was that he had changed a lot over the five weeks.

He described the programme as fun, enjoyable, amazing and life-changing.

He said that he had really enjoyed the experience and had so much fun. I knew that this young man would still have a journey of ups and downs, but he now had the tools and techniques that would empower him to take those challenges head-on and come out smiling. He could make changes in his life and know it is the right thing for him. As I wished him well moving forward, he ran at me and threw his arms around me. He said, "Thank you for believing in me and listening to what I want out of life. You have changed me forever and I will never forget you." I just had a small teeny tiny adjustment to his last sentence. I told him that I did not change him, I just showed him what to do. He was the one who put it in to practise and made those changes a reality.

Have I mentioned that I love what I do!

Case Study Number 6

By Julianne Hadden

Reason for referral from point of contact in school

Bob   10 years old   Boy   England

Bob was referred to the Jepeca programme to help him with his relationship with his mother. He had a temper and his behaviour at school had been deteriorating for the last two or three years. My point of contact, in this case the head teacher, had spent many hours with Bob, and yet his behaviour persisted, as did the disrespect he showed towards staff and his mother.

Bob had another year in primary school before moving up to secondary school, and the disruption caused by his refusal to conform would impact the whole class's exam results and their ability to absorb the curriculum. Other parents had complained about his behaviour, and something had to be done.

The head teacher at this school was forward-thinking and had heard of the results we were achieving. When he invited me to meet, initially he had hoped I would do some workshops or group work with a group of children that had developed friendship issues. Although he was disappointed that we do not engage in workshops or group work, he understood that we felt that the individual needs of the child would not be met, and therefore the success of the work would be jeopardised.

Session 1 – Initial Assessment

Bob came into the room to meet me with a serious scowl on his face. He was not happy to be singled out to attend this programme, not happy at all! As I started to explain about the following weeks and the fact that my own children had done the programme, he became more relaxed. He asked me if my children had problems and I told him that everybody has some sort of challenges that can be described as a problem, if that is the word you choose to use. At some point in life, everyone will encounter challenges and I wanted my children to be able to overcome those challenges happily and to make any changes they wish, effortlessly. Yeah, he thought, I want that... and so we began...

Bob was a very intelligent boy. He had a shock of blonde hair that could almost be described as white, and thick black glasses. He sat excitedly now, watching me turn every page of my consultation pack, eager to start.

Going through the questionnaire, it became apparent that Bob wanted to work on his behaviour. Amazing that a 10-year-old can identify that his behaviour was causing him a problem. His school had identified that his behaviour was a problem and his family had identified that hid behaviour was a problem, yet his behaviour was still a problem!

I love it when the client identify what others have identified, not because they have been told it is, but because they know and feel it is a problem. Sometimes I will ask them 'how' they know it is a problem if I think that they are giving me an answer they think I want to hear. I have yet to come across a client that pretends. Normally they are genuinely looking for a way to move forward, or 'how to' move forward. If they do not want to be there, they are not shy about saying so. You can bring a horse to water, but you cannot make them drink.

The goal he decided was to work on his behaviour and manage his feelings. He told me in great detail how his behaviour was causing lots of trouble, especially at home. Bob loved his mum but somehow always managed to annoy her, which in turn would annoy him, and before he knew it, he would be shouting that he hated her. Needless to say, later he was sorry. But it was tiring and he could see the cycle shining through.

Bob got on really well with his dad and spent many hours with him. He felt a great need to protect his family and this had been the root of some of the problems in school. When peers would shout and call his family names, he would think he needed to protect them, and so began the cycle. Fight, get in to trouble in school, and then return to normal until someone called his family names again.

By the end of the first session, Bob was very excited about the future sessions. Before he left the room, he came over to where I was sitting, stretched out his hand, looked me in the eye and shook my hand firmly. He told me that he thought that the Jepeca programme would really help him. I could not agree more. He turned to leave and as he closed the door, he knocked on the door, excitedly, and waved. Then he left, came back and did it again! Funny.

Session 2 - Filters

This session came a little too late in some ways, but perfect in others. Bob had been to a sports day and there had been an incident that was reported to the head teacher from the head of another school that revolved around Bob's behaviour. As soon as I arrived at the school, my point of contact updated me and was very disappointed. I reassured them that we would work on it today.

Bob came in appearing full of confidence and sat down ready for our session. I asked the usual... what was the best and worst thing that happened to him since I saw him last? Interestingly, he was looking forward to his family holiday at half-term to Disney World Florida. He was going to his friend's house after school and he had been promised a new Xbox game. And the worst thing? After thinking long and hard, nothing. OK! So I told him that I spoke to the head teacher and they were not happy with an incident that happened yesterday. Bob just shook his head and said, "It is all sorted". Interesting. On further exploration of "all sorted," I discovered that he sorted it out himself and had moved on, even though his mother had been informed and the head teacher had a stern word with him. It just did not seem to register with him or faze him how serious the incident was! He would do his detention and life would go on.

I asked him to tell me what happened. In his words, there was a group of 10 and 11 year olds who were making him look and feel stupid so he put them in their place. He said what he had to say to shut them up. Right, that makes sense; I told him I could see why he did what he did, but how had that worked out for him? On reflection, he thought things could have worked out better. If he did not lose his temper, if he did what he was told, instead of answering back and being cheeky, or if he walked away.

Well it was perfect for today's session so he could understand the process. The shock on his face was comical.

"You mean, you are not angry with me?"

"No, I think you can learn tons of things from that incident yesterday, and it is perfect for today's session," although I did mention that I did not want him going out looking for examples to use every week during sessions!

So I went through the bubble and proved he had the bubble. He pretended that he was not bothered but as I got closer, he leaned back. We did laugh a lot during this part of the session. Next, we personalised it and that I shall keep between us, on this occasion. Suffice to say, it was like Bob; unique, fantastic and fun.

The next part was to put the bubble to use, and this is always a bit tricky when the client has such strong feelings towards the other person involved. For Bob, it was the fact that he had to play the part of a girl, who made fun of him and resulted in everyone getting angry yet again. I understood but I asked him to be open to what I was asking of him, as it was really important that he got the other people's perspective. Long pause, and then, "OK".

As I played the part of Bob, I needed to know what was going for him at that moment in time and he was more than happy to provide this information. Next, I gave him the dude, and the role play began. As Bob began to launch the dude at me, I caught every word and threw it back, using the words that he had told me earlier. This continued on for a while. Eventually, it came to a standstill. So how did it feel being the most significant other? Happy, powerful and popular, he told me. I told him that I did not feel too good being him. It was almost like I was trying to keep up with whatever she said and I did not feel good. I was sad and angry, but mostly frustrated. He was nodding as I said all of the above.

Next, we did the role play again, but this time I was using the bubble that Bob had personalised so that he could see what it was like from the perspective of the other person involved. Totally different story! Bob followed me around doing his best to take me out with the dude, but I was doing my own thing and not giving him any reaction. Very quickly, he tired of shouting abuse at me and said that he wanted to stop. When I asked him how it felt this time being the girl involved, he said it was awful. He could not believe how stupid she felt. She felt sad and annoyed, but mostly she felt like an idiot. As for me being Bob, it felt fantastic. I couldn't hear a word that was being said and I felt happy and in control. Brilliant. I could see that Bob was smiling as he listened to me.

Before I moved on to the next part, I asked him if he understood what had happened. The girl was angry and annoyed, and was looking for someone to bounce off. She wanted to make someone as angry and annoyed as she felt. Once she had identified Bob, she made her move. Whether she took her time or whether it was a spur of the moment thing does not really matter. What matters is that she wanted to make someone else feel as she did. She was looking for a reaction and what had he provided her with? A reaction. He had provided a reaction every time. So she was in control. The look on his face as the penny dropped and he understood what filtering was all about was priceless. "Oh my God," he said, and he sat down. I left him to think it through and he took his time. Eventually, he said, "I have been reacting to people the whole time." I simply nodded and smiled as he continued to make sense of what had just happened.

This time, I was the girl and Bob was himself, but with his bubble. He played his part perfectly. No matter what I said as I threw the dude, Bob simple used his bubble, found a distraction and remained in control. Perfect. I used the words that he had said earlier so that we could keep it real. I was so proud of him. Eventually, I said I had enough and he had the biggest smile. "That was brilliant, I really did not hear what you were saying."

How amazing was that? He talked non-stop for about 10 minutes. Then he turned to me and said, "Thank you". I finished the session and told him it can be used for past, present or future situations.

That day was very special for Bob and I know he will take this experience with him wherever he goes. I have no doubt that it changed his life. I could see it in his face and his eyes and his smile. The realisation that his reaction was fuelling her behaviour was the influence that I mentioned. You cannot change anyone, but you can influence them by your reaction! It's all good. As Bob left to go to break, he shook my hand excitedly, went out the door, waved, came back to the door and waved again. Happy days.

Session 3 – Thought Training and Development

This week, Bob was full of chat as he told me (before I asked) about the many different ways that his bubble had been used. He even tried to tell a younger child in Year Three how to use it as he was sad and felt that people were picking on him. How times had changed! There was so much energy in this young man. It just needed pointing in a direction and a way that would work for him.

I had a good report from the school this week and, pleasantly, he had not been in the head teacher's office, which was also unusual!

This week's session was on thinking and the importance of training and developing thoughts. What surprised me was that when I asked Bob how he thought that we make our thoughts real, he actually answered me as if he had read the manual! I was shocked and asked him he had been talking with someone who had completed the programme. He had not, but interestingly for some of the sessions, I find that clients know what they to do but do not know 'how to' do it on demand. Now I was about to tell him.

He enjoyed the session and had plans for each of his thoughts. Bob was a very bright boy and he planned to use this information to get a good job. As I went through each part of the session, he was particularly interested in how he could use it for his future. So that is what we did.

I asked him what he would like to be or do when he left school. Bob had already decided he was going to start his own business, like is father's, which was a paint wholesalers. What would he need to do to make it a reality? We worked through the steps he had taken to date, the steps he intended to take in the near future, and those that he would take over the next few years.

With the negative thoughts, he could understand how saying he can't do something would make a difference to the end result, as he regularly says it in English lessons and this gets him in to trouble. I showed him how to flip it over and stop himself as soon as he starts to realise that he is saying it. That was going to be put to use this afternoon, he told me excitedly. He did not have any other thoughts that were negative, so we moved on.

It is hard to believe that this boy was only 10 years old. He was so focused. Sometimes I could see in his face wonder and charm like that of a little boy on Christmas morning as he discovered that Santa had been and left him everything on his wish list. But at other times, his maturity and use of words and his thought process was staggering.

Bob was, and is, a delight. He reminded me at the end of every session to come and see him again next week with the next instalment. Again, he shook my hand, waved at the door and returned to wave again before returning to class.

Session 4 - Emotional Awareness

The head teacher approached me as I opened the front door to the school and took me to one side. He told me he was very pleased with Bob's progress and that his class teacher asked if it were possible to work with everyone in Year Five, including herself. You may laugh, but it is not the first time we have been asked to work with teachers!

I was halfway through the sessions. It was just as important for Bob to complete the emotional awareness and communication weeks even though he had made such huge leaps forward. I asked him how he had got on in the last week. He felt like it was all working, especially at football practise as some of the boys could get more caught up in the importance of the score rather than the importance of teamwork. Bob told me, "You have to keep the mind positive, you know!"

He was not using the bubble as much as he did as after the bubble session. The reason was that he did not need to, but he did visualise future football games at night occasionally, as some teams were harder than others to play. Moving forward with the emotional awareness session, Bob took his place beside me at the whiteboard. As I explained the traffic lights, he nodded slowly, taking it all in. When I explained about the RAG, he asked me to wait a minute. I looked at him as he redrew what was on the board.

"Right, got it! You can move on now." I smiled and asked if he had any questions. "No I've worked it out myself, it makes sense now."

I wanted to let Bob know that should something creep past the bubble, then it would flag up on the traffic lights. From here, he could recognise what feeling it was and decide what he wanted to do with it. For example, if during the football game one of the other team called him a name and it got through the bubble, he would know because his feelings would give him a signal in the form of a specific feeling. Then he could use the RAG, rather than lose it (which became his new mantra!), and find a way of moving forward that would work for him. Going through all the options that were available to him, he mentioned that he used to punch them if they got too annoying but now he knows that it would not work out for him so he uses the bubble and this would be a good back-up plan. Simples.

We worked through another few examples of when, where and how he could use the RAG. He had a young cousin that would come around to his house and drive him mad. He would take all of his stuff out and had broken some precious cars in the past. When he complained to his mother, she would just tell him he had loads more and them Bob would get more annoyed until he lost it. This had become a cycle and he hated his cousin coming around now, even though he had not broken anything for a long time. Using the traffic lights and the RAG, Bob could see that if he did not do something different, he would lose it again and get in to trouble with his mum. The cycle was so obvious. We worked on his list of options, and eventually he decided on writing a letter to ask his mum to protect his precious cars that he had minded from when he was a baby.

I got Bob to stand back and take stock. What did he notice? I love that question. It is so open, yet it allows the client to come from absolutely anywhere.

"Well," he said, "I think we have done a lot of work today. I wish I knew this when I was younger." He also mentioned that the feelings he had when he was in English lessons had changed. He could identify this by using his traffic light. Before he would be feeling anxious and feel stupid but now he was feeling positive and relaxed.

Coming to the end of this session, I mentioned that we had two more left. Bob wanted to continue after the six sessions but I assured him that he knew all that he needed to know; it was just putting it in to practise now. Practise was not difficult for Bob as he was focused. Remember, the more use it, the less you need it. Strange, but true.

Before he left, Bob took a seat beside me and asked me if I would miss him when we had finished the sessions. "Of course," I said, "but I look forward to hearing about your successes in the future." He smiled and shook my hand, walked to the door, waved and left. Then he returned to the door, knocked and waved again, really excitedly. :)

Session 5 - Communication

Bob, Bob, Bob.

Ever ready, full of excitement and full of life. Bob was telling me all about his week and the best thing that happened to him, which was winning his football match on Sunday, before I even got into the room. He could not thing of a worst thing, so could we please start the session!

As this was the penultimate session, I asked him to teach me all that he had learned in the last few weeks. "Pretend I am new and do not know anything; where would you start?"

Bob indicated for me to sit where he usually did and to watch what he was doing. He continued to draw the different parts of the session and talked his way skilfully through the programme. I was impressed at his knowledge, but not surprised. After all, he appeared to know what to do to get things done. Now he knew 'how to' as well.

When he had finished, I applauded. "Well done, young man! That was perfect! Now, let's talk communication, or should I say, let's communicate! So the question is, how do we communicate? How do you know when someone is annoyed?" We discussed words, body language and tone. Nothing was too much for this young man.

I thought it might be useful for Bob to be able to look at things from a different perspective so we looked at the incident that happened at the sports day. Standing him in the middle of the room, I got him to identify where his problem was (towards the wall), and what and where he would put the outcome (by the window). Then I asked him to take a step in the direction of his problem, as he described it and spoke about it, why he had it etc. Then turning him to the window where the light was, I asked him to explore what he would like to happen instead, and how it could make it happen. He really enjoyed this. It did not take him long to realise the different feelings that the different directions were associated with. He much preferred the outcome side. "More fun," I think, were the words he used.

Finishing the session, I asked if he had any questions. "Not today," Bob said, and stood up to shake my hand. He looked back smiling as he walked to the door, opened it and stood on the other side waving excitedly. Then, as per usual, he walked off but came back to knock on the door again with a final wave.

As I was writing up my notes, I saw that he had left me a little hand written note. "Thank you :)"

Session 6 – Final Assessment

This was my final week. Bob came in and immediately gave me a little box of chocolates, which he had bought with his own money, and a 'Thank you' card. How sweet. I asked him what the best thing and worst thing that had happened since I saw him last.

"Well, that is easy," he said. "The best was seeing you, and the worst is not seeing you next week…" Mind you, he was smiling as he said it, so I think he knew he was being cute.

As this was our last week, he was prepared to go over the paperwork again. Every week is different and we do stress that if the client misses a week, we cannot catch up on the missed session. Bob had attended all of the sessions and everyone noticed the change.

Starting on the feedback, Bob said that he enjoyed the bubble as it explained a lot. He found that it had taught him things about life's difficulties and 'how to' do something about them. He uses it when he needs it.

The Jepeca programme had helped him with family issues. He said that his mum is not upset now because he does not ignore her when she calls him. He also said it has helped with his behaviour in school as when he gets mad with someone, he now thinks about the steps. He had an example of this that he used with his friend a few days before. They were both wanting to take a free kick in football, so Bob turned to his friend and said, "Why are we fighting? Let's work this out," and that is exactly what happened.

When asked if he had noticed a difference since completing the Jepeca programme, he said he felt that he'd got happier.

His mum had noticed a difference, especially when she collects him after school, and she also says that he's happier. "She is enjoying spending time with me now." Bob told me that he and his mother had made plans to go out to the park once a week, just the two of them.

His teachers had also noticed a difference and even the head teacher spoke to him a few days previously to congratulate him on not being flagged up for behaviour, although he did say that he missed seeing him, which Bob though rather funny.

He described the Jepeca programme as great, exciting and helpful. He had noticed that his behaviour in school had improved and he now makes people happier. He likes to play a lot now and he is happy with his life. When asked if he could think of anything to improve the sessions, he thought for a bit, then said, "No, I enjoyed all of them a lot. They have a lot of use."

At the end of this session, Bob shook my hand and left as usual, waving at the door, only to return four times to wave to me, before he returned to class. He did make me smile, and still does.

Bob has a very bright future ahead of him. This could have turned out so differently. He was very luck to have a forward-thinking head teacher to support him.

Case Study Number 7

By Katie Dommett

Reason for referral from point of contact in school

Matthew   14 years old   Boy   England

Matthew had been referred to me on a number of different issues. His behaviour in class had been deteriorating and Matthew seemed unable to take any responsibility for his actions when challenged by the teachers. He also lacked confidence and had low self-esteem, and when I read his background notes, I began to gain a clearer picture of the many 'bumps' he had already faced in his life.

Matthew had been in care on and off since birth, and while several different families for short spells of time had fostered him, he had only recently been placed with a family that looked like they would be adopting him. He was under the care of social workers and had been to 10 different primary schools, and this was his third secondary school at the age of 14. He had been seeing a counsellor for the past couple of years but the school had major concerns and felt he was heading down a slippery slope where the outcome would be yet more heartache and trouble. They said that Matthew had no real friends at school and seemed unable to form lasting relationships. In secondary school, this is a major thing as peer groups become established and teenagers begin to work out their own identity and individuality. This then seemed to impact him in his progression academically and they were concerned for his upcoming exams. They had described Matthew as a concern and a child/young person who looked sad and distressed a lot of the time. The school felt that if they did not have a successful intervention, then Matthew's future looked very bleak.

Session 1 - Initial Assessment

When I met with Matthew on this first session, I felt a real sense of sadness and desperation from him. As he entered the room, his shoulders were hunched over and he seemed nervous to make eye contact, as if I was maybe there to tell him off. I knew he had experiences with counselling and other therapies with little positive outcome, so his body language told me that he wanted to be convinced that I would be something different to what he had already experienced. Rapport building is vital in this first session, as we need to gain trust very quickly. I focus on empathy and looking for ways to enter the child's inner world and validate their thoughts and feelings. They need to hear that the way they feel is normal and valid, and should not be dismissed or belittled. For Matthew, this seemed very important as he told me that he has been told to get on with things and make the best of bad situations. He felt that this was not solving the problem for him.

I felt it was really important for Matthew to understand what would be happening in the following sessions. He loved the fact that we had structure, different techniques each week and that we would have an end date. It was at this point he mentioned how he had been in counselling for a couple of years with little improvement and was bored with discussing the same things over and over. He openly admitted that he didn't like how he was and he wanted to change, but he couldn't see how that could happen.

We started to complete the initial questionnaire and I began to realise that Matthew liked to be mobile in sessions; he seemed agitated sitting so I told him he could walk around or write on the board while I asked questions. He seemed genuinely amazed that I had given him permission to do this and seemed to relax slightly more, looking at me rather than at the floor.

Once I started to ask Matthew questions, he came across as answering very honestly and openly. He stated in a very matter of fact way that he had been in and out of care and that he had only recently been settled with permanent foster parents. He even seemed slightly proud when he told me that he had been to so many schools. When I asked him how he felt about that, he replied, "It's just the way it is, I suppose". His body language and tone did not match what he was saying at all. He answered with sadness in his voice and a sadness that seemed to encompass his body. He was almost in a foetal position when he returned back to his seat, hunched up with his knees nearly to his chest, as if this would give him some comfort. Comfort maybe he had never experienced.

He described his home life as "better". I followed up with asking, "Better than what?" He explained that now he was at a more permanent home, he felt more settled, so this seemed better than him being moved around. He did say that this had happened before though and then he had been moved, so he hoped this wouldn't be the case again. When I asked him if he was happy, he said he didn't. When I asked him what would make him happier, he talked about being with his currently family and for his experience in school with other children and in his lessons to be happier. He said he felt unloved and unwanted and when I asked him whom he liked spending time with he replied, "No one". He had no idea what to do with his feelings and said that he often got upset and angry with people and this always led to him getting in to trouble. He told me he was on school report. When I asked what he thought would happen at the end of this report, he said, "Probably suspended. No one really cares about me anyway so it won't make any difference". He had such low self-esteem that he truly believed that he didn't matter and that no one would miss him if he weren't around. He really believed this and admitted that nothing so far in his life had proved him otherwise. He spoke about how his birth parents hadn't wanted him and that pattern had followed with everywhere he had gone since then. He could not begin to believe that could be different, or that if he felt better about himself, things around him would feel differently too.

Matthew was small for his age and I remember looking at this young man and feeling that he looked and displayed the actions of someone much younger but with the weight of the world on his shoulders. The great thing about this first session was that Matthew wanted to work with me and actually asked me if I would be the person that would help him finally. It took a lot to hold back from crying at that point as I realised I was probably the first person in a long time, if not ever, that was able to look him in the eye and tell him that as long as he wanted to, I would be able to help him with all of the things he was worried about. It was an amazing moment.

Session 2 - Filters

When Matthew came back in the following week, I was already noticing a difference. The sadness was slowly seeping away from his face and body, and in its place I began to see excitement and intrigue in to what the sessions were about and what he would learn from them. He came into the room looking at me and talked about how he had thought about what this session would be about, as I had said we were doing "the bubble". Matthew then asked if we would be doing any drama in our sessions. He explained how he loved drama and acting out and he found it really helpful. This is an important note to remember; all children are different and may find more artistic ways (art, drama, role play, analogies) to support the understanding of the techniques. As long as the technique is delivered correctly, the practise part can be adapted to incorporate the above.

As I began to explain the bubble to him and we worked through the nice and not-so-nice things that had been said to him, I began to enter into Matthew's inner world. He would use words such as four-eyes (he wore glasses), retard, idiot, dick, loser, loner, and so on. When we practised the bubble, we focused on utilising the Jepeca Cycle to show Matthew that if he continued to react and respond as he had, then his outcome would remain the same. This allowed Matthew to try different responses using the bubble and then putting that in the cycle to see the change in his outcome. He came to his own conclusions that by using the bubble and responding with either doing something else, talking to someone else, or answering his foster parents/teacher with a suitable response, he was able to control a positive outcome for himself. We worked through so many different scenarios of times with his teachers, his foster parents, other kids at school and outside of school, and his enthusiasm spilled over as he wanted to act each one out in lots of different ways. I asked him how he was feeling and he answered, "Back in control". I could see him stand just that little bit taller, and after going through any particular scenario, he would want to talk through what he had done, how it had made him feel and how that was so different to what he had done before. I felt the adrenaline rush as he gained excitement, and at one point, I even heard a little, "Wow," leave his lips. He assured me when we finished that session, he would be practising the bubble all week.

Session 3 - Thought Training and Development

Matthew walked in on session three with his chest puffed out and an announcement to make."I've stopped the counselling. I've spoken to my social worker and I have said I don't want to continue".

I looked at him and he looked please as punch! I said, "That's great that you have made such a confident decision. What made you decide that?"

Matthew looked at me and said, "You are the first person who has actually paid me any real attention and explained things to me in a way that it can help me. At counselling, I have talked about the same thing for nearly two years with no way forward, but last week I left you knowing how to change something about my life for the better. I love Jepeca!"

Now, currently inside I was doing a major victory dance and whooping and hollering, but I looked at Matthew and said, "I'm really pleased that you have looked at something going on in your life, thought about what it is doing for you and made a decision that gives you a better outcome. Well done!" It made me even happier to think that we were now going to look at Matthew's thoughts and how he can make anything he wants a reality and how empowering that will be.

Now he felt more control of what he let in and out, he could focus on making things happen for him and dealing with different issues he had happening with working in class and also how he felt about his future. He felt that, due to his challenging start, it would have a negative impact on his future. The part in thought training where we STOP the negative thoughts and flip them to positive ones, was imperative for Matthew's development, and for him to understand how he can make these experiences work for him. We talked about people that inspired him and their life stories, and how people do come from every walk of life and how the choices they make and the steps they take towards making their lives better are in their control. Matthew seemed to really take this on board and said he wanted to go home and research his favourite actors and read their life stories. We also used the thought training to look at future goals for Matthew. He wants to be an actor and go to drama school, so he began to look at how he could make that a reality for himself. We carried on with thought training, showing Matthew how he could create a positive and permanent change in his life if he wanted to, and he seemed amazed and enthralled. These were life skills that he had never been aware of and he now looked like a boy who had been let loose in a sweet shop. He had already been one step ahead of me with the decision about the counselling and I felt so proud.

Session 4 - Emotional Awareness

Matthew came in to this week's session happy and smiling, and even mentioned before we started that we didn't have many sessions left. He explained how he had been using his bubble at school when other kids were being nasty, but also using it when dealing with his mum and dad, and filtering what he wanted to take in. He seemed so excited to tell me about all these different occasions where he had put it in to practise and also talked about how he had taken steps to improve his behaviour in class. He explained how he had thought about how he would sometimes try and distract other kids in the class, but in the last week he had thought about the cycle of doing this, how it didn't end up working out well for him, and so he took different steps and listened in class and focused on his own work. He showed me his report card, which had lots of smiley faces and, "Well done," written on it; he was so proud of this.

Once I had explained emotional awareness and the traffic lights, we began acting out different choices to all these scenarios he had. He came up with times where he was angry in class, when he was being asked to do something he didn't really want to do, where someone was being mean to him in the playground, and when he simply felt lonely. Matthew felt so empowered that he could see the results of his choices and how that would impact the recipient. He enjoyed coming up with a real variety of choices including hurting the person, laying traps for them, hiding his clothes under his bed when asked to tidy his room, and blaming the mess on his pets! I really saw a wonderful imagination and ability to fantasise in Matthew, and made sure I told him this. It felt more like a drama class than a coaching session, but it was so much fun. We were acting out the good, bad and ugly choices so he could get a really sense of how he can create his own reality and, depending on the choice he makes, how amazing that can be. He had a real light bulb moment towards the end where he looked at me and said, "I'm actually quite powerful and the actions I choose are powerful too. Wow!" Matthew really understood in this session how, when he begins to feel differently about something, he has the choice to do something that will give him the best outcome or he can choose to do something that can leave him feeling worse and the only person who truly influences that is himself. Again, he left the session saying he would be practising this new technique all week. It seemed to empower Matthew so much to actually have tools and techniques that he could take away from our session and use immediately.

Session 5 - Communication

Matthew came in to the session today with great news. He wanted to tell me about a part in a play that he had gone for in the week since I had last worked with him and how happy he was that he had got the part. He explained how he had to read for it in front of the drama class but how he had thought about how he was going to do it before and then made it a reality for himself by putting the steps in place. He practised the part in the days leading up to it and asked for help from some of his "new friends", as he liked to put it! He didn't have anything bad to report on the previous week, and when I asked him if he noticed a difference in himself, he said that he felt happy and things seemed more fun and interesting now. He enjoyed coming to school and he enjoyed being at home. Both of which, he said, were new feelings for him.

Our penultimate session was a real pulling together of everything Matthew had learnt over the previous four weeks. Teachers had already begun to feedback to me that they could see a real improvement in Matthew in lessons and a sense of responsibility being taken in class for his own learning. Matthew had begun to mention that he had made some friends and felt more confident at lunchtime to sit and chat with some of the lads in his year. We explored different ways of communicating and how that can be received, and again he looked at how his responses to his teachers and foster parents could leave him feeling pretty low or angry. He saw how the outward behaviour and tone doesn't always match and mirror what's going on inside and that can be said for everyone, not just him. He really 'got' this and began to look at how he could phrase things differently or use his body language differently. The drama came out again and it was great to see him being so expressive.

I saw a different boy stood in front of me in that session. I saw a boy who wanted to own a stage and who wanted to display how expressive he was. This was a newfound confidence and his visible happiness felt infectious. I felt as if I could see inside his head to see lots of different cogs now turning in sync with each other and, as a result, everything was coming together for this young man and life, and the future seemed not only positive, but also exciting and exhilarating.

Session 6 - Final Assessment

Even though I love week six as it gives the client the opportunity to give their feedback openly, I'd be lying if I said that I wasn't a little sad about our final session together. I had seen such a change in Matthew and part of me wanted to remain that little fly on the wall to see him progress and achieve the potential he now knew he could reach.

When I began to ask him the questions about how things felt differently now and what that was, I was amazed by how confidently he spoke. "I have friends now, I feel settled in the classroom, I'm not being disruptive anymore, I'm taking more responsibility for myself, I like myself now."

When we moved on to the final questionnaire, the results were outstanding. Matthew had gone from someone who felt sad, lonely, depressed and not knowing what to do with this, to someone who stood before me now with a part in the school play, friends within class and a newfound sense of responsibility for his future, and for his behaviour. Matthew had been actively using all the techniques, and in particular now the RAG, where he acknowledged the change on feeling and then looked at his choices and options in how he would deal with that feeling. He even said to me, "I know that my feelings are just signals to me now and it's what I do with them that counts". I love my job!

Matthew had thrown away the 'crutches' of counselling and, I think, made a decision for the first time in his life that gave him a real positive outcome. He had used the Jepeca programme to make key decisions in only six short weeks and these decisions, I knew, would help shape his future for him. It left me feeling incredibly proud of the young man Matthew had become, and when he said to me that I had helped to change his life, it left me with a feeling of such satisfaction.

Matthew was now a young man taking responsibility for his actions, acknowledging his feelings and making sound decisions based on this. He was someone who was able to communicate effectively with his peers and also respond appropriately to those in authority. He was coming off report and his teachers were incredibly proud of the changes he had made. This, as Matthew put it, was down to the Jepeca programme.

**"Lucy said that her mum had noticed
a major difference
and had told Lucy that she loved Jepeca
and what it had done for her."**

Case Study Number 8

By Katie Dommett

Reason for referral from point of contact in school

Lucy   11 years old   Girl   England

Lucy had been referred to Jepeca for a variety of reasons. She'd had it pretty rough in a very short space of time. In the last 12 months, one of her grandparents had died, and she had been experiencing bullying at school from two children in particular. Mainly verbal bullying, but there had been evidence of physical bullying on occasion, which had been dealt with by the school, but I felt concerned that this may have still been continuing. Her parents had split up quite suddenly and she was living with her mum and brother (who had recently been diagnosed with autism). She had also been sharing a room with her brother, who had been recorded as being verbally abusive to Lucy, as well as physically violent. He had been hitting her and pinning her to the floor on several occasions. The understanding from the point of contact was that the mother had now looked at moving them in to separate bedrooms but at the time of working with Lucy, I was unaware if this had actually been done. Her self-esteem was at an all-time low and she was two terms away from going to secondary school, so the school were really focused on Lucy getting the support they felt she needed.

The point of contact described Lucy as a child who was not coping with the vast amount of changes that had happened, and as I mentioned earlier, they had noticed considerable change in her in the way she walked around the school, participated in class and her general appearance. She had lost any emotion in her eyes and looked 'vacant'. The worry was that without any type of intervention, Lucy's coping mechanisms would not be sufficient to deal with all the changes and this would impact her in her behaviour, approach to school and relationships, and could lead to a very destructive path. This is seen so many times in other children where they have been abandoned at critical periods in their life, and as a result, drugs, food, alcohol, promiscuous behaviour and destructive relationships (to mention a few) become far more appealing and something that the individual feels they can control. I was really looking forward to Lucy and helping her with all of these changes that had occurred in her young life.

Session 1 - Initial assessment

When Lucy walked into the room, I likened her to a startled deer. She had these large doe eyes that darted around the room and it seemed as if she had an imaginary force pushing her towards me in the room. The resistance on the first session was electric, and although she seemed happy to be with me, she had no idea why and said that no one had explained to her about me or the programme she was about to undertake. She seemed incredibly sad and resigned to something that I can only describe as depressing. It seemed as if she had nothing to live for or no incentive to be anything other than sad and quiet. I began to explain who I was and what the Jepeca programme was. I really focused on reinforcing to Lucy how I could help her and how after we had gone through all the 'boring bits' of form filling this week, we would begin learning new techniques, which would be lots of fun and helpful for her. I saw a very small glimmer of interest at this point and started to complete the first forms, looking to build more rapport.

Interestingly, when I asked her what her hobbies and interest were, she said art immediately. I asked her to tell me more about that and I could see her shoulders begin to drop down and she seemed to relax slightly more in to the chair. It was something she felt comfortable talking about and I felt it important before moving on to more serious topics; it was necessary for Lucy to feel more relaxed as she clearly had not been briefed at all about me or what we were going to do. She spoke about her passion for drawing and how she felt she could 'escape' when she drew and how it helped her with expressing her feelings at any particular time. I asked her if she would like to draw while she was working with me and she could present it back to me at the end of the programme. I explained that she could draw whatever came to her while we worked together and I would love to see her work at the end of it. She agreed and seemed happy at being asked to do this. We then moved on to the initial questionnaire.

She told me in that first session that she hated herself and that she was ugly. She said it with no emotion, only a resignation that in her world that was a factual comment and something that no one could dispute. Lucy had no goals, no dreams, and no aspirations. The only thing Lucy liked was being on her own, and when I asked her how she would describe herself, she said, "Weird". When I asked her what she would like to gain out of the sessions, she simply said, "To be happier". When she spoke about her home life, and her brother in particular, she described it as, "Being all about Tyler," and that she didn't really feature at home at the moment with everything going on with him. At this first session, she didn't really mention her grandparent passing or the bullying in any great detail, other than she had issues with some of the kids in the class which had been going on forever (as she put it). This often happens where the schools will give us a lot of information and in the first session that doesn't always all come out. It isn't necessary for the programme to be fully effective but what I have found is that normally by week two or three, the child feels able to disclose more and more and all sorts of disclosures will then come to fruition. I really felt Lucy's pain on that first session and it did sit with me after the session had ended, which doesn't always happen. I think it is in part to do with the sadness I saw on her face. Such sadness for someone so young.

Session 2 - Filters

Lucy walked in to our next session more like a slightly shocked rabbit! The eyes had calmed and she seemed warmer, and I even saw a hint of a smile when I reiterated how this was the start of me helping her to change so many things in her life. I would constantly reaffirm with Lucy throughout our work together how great she was and how she had made the best decision continuing to work with me and how I was going to help her with so many different issues. I could say there was a 'mantra' of sorts going on but I felt it was important for Lucy to hear that same consistent message week in, week out that I was there solely to help her and to show her how she could empower herself and take control of her life.

The bubble worked so well for Lucy and she impressed me greatly with her ability to imagine the bubble. When we moved on to the visualising of the bubble, she asked if she would be doing this as herself or as the third person! I admit it took me a minute to reply to this and I explained that it would be better for her to visualise herself in the bubble if she felt able too. She immediately closed her eyes and began to describe this beautiful and vivid rainbow coloured bubble that she was loving being in and how she would physically reach out with her eyes shut to show me where her bubble was. She had been experiencing bullying from two main children in class and it had been slowly chipping away at her. We put in to practise immediately the different scenarios. It became clear that there was a boy and girl that had been bullying Lucy. As she began to throw the balls, the words began to flow: ugly, weirdo, loser, idiot, loner, ugly cow, etc. Then sentences began to form, "You have a nutter for a brother, and you are so ugly, no one is ever going to like you!" The balls were coming thick and fast, and her voice began to get louder and more aggressive as she really began to see herself as the bully. She carried on for quite some time and then simply stopped and looked at me and said, "I'm done". I asked her how she had felt as the bully, and she said she had felt in control and fed off the fact that I looked more and more upset as she threw the balls.

We then did it with me having the bubble up, and, to give her credit, she began again with the same enthusiasm! She did, however, stop fairly soon after starting, and when I asked her why she had stopped so quickly, she replied, "It got boring. I wasn't getting any reaction". I saw the little light go on in her head as she began to realise the impact of the bubble and how much of a difference it makes. She worked so hard, and after we had acted out her using the bubble, she smiled. I asked her how she felt after that particular time, and she replied, "I felt so much better but I felt so sorry for you". As I had been the bully, I asked her why she felt sorry for me. She replied, "Well you seemed so angry and frustrated and I felt really good, and I just wanted you to feel a bit better about yourself". Wow...

Session 3 - Thought Training and Development

I can only describe this session as amazing. Up until this point, I had Lucy's background from the teachers, but she had yet to disclose much more other than the bullying, her brother and her own self-esteem issues. As massive as that had already been, she had still not let me in to her home life or recent experiences of loss.

We began to work on the thought training and I asked her to take me through the steps of a time where she wanted to do something and she actually did do it. She talked about when she had wanted to go to a friend's house for a sleepover and how she actually did do it. We started working through the thoughts and making it real and when we finished, she said to me, "That was strange when I went to Alice's house". I asked her why and then BANG! She disclosed that she had gone for the sleepover because her grandparent had died and how her friend and friend's mum had known this information, but no one had told her and she felt very angry about this. She then said that her parents had split up and how that had been difficult and how she didn't see her dad as much and that hurt.

The whole time, the main thread remained the same; a real sense and feeling of loss that she did not know what the hell to do about and how it left her feeling so empty, sad and alone. We then spent the rest of the session looking specifically at this and how when she feels this way, we can 'stop' and flip it in to a positive feeling and look at all the positives surrounding that experience. I needn't have worried about Lucy grasping this, as she was more than able to give me lots of positives around each of these situations and what has been gained as a result of this. She talked about spending quality time with her parents now and how they might be happier if they weren't together and this would benefit her. She talked about how her grandparent had been really old and quite poorly so at least they were at rest now and she could always draw pictures and write letters or a diary to express how she was feeling. She left the room that day smiling and had even made a little song up about "stopping and flipping the feeling!"

Session 4 - Emotional Awareness

I could have cried when I saw Lucy walk in at the next session. She came bounding in like a spring lamb with the broadest grin, and it was the first time I could say that she looked happy since we had begun work together. Emotional awareness was so positive for Lucy. She looked at her change in feelings, especially when she felt shy or upset, and we looked at all the wide range of choices available to her. It still makes me giggle when I think about her particular reaction to what can be seen as poor choices. An example was where she said she felt frustrated when another girl starting picking on her. We looked at what she could do about it and when I threw in the choice of, "You could pull her hair, and punch and kick her?" she looked visibly mortified! I did follow up with the fact that, although it may not be the choice she would go for, it is still a choice.

She said, "I would never do that. That would mean I would get in to so much trouble and I would hurt her". Bingo! The realisation that she has the control to decide the best possible outcome. The choices are all there, but it is the one that will lead her back to green that will always win. It was also in this session that she said that she felt different. I asked her if she knew how she felt different and she simply said that things seemed better in her life and she already seemed happier. The wonderful part to this is that it was also written all over her face.

Session 5 - Communication

When Lucy came in for her next session on communication, it seemed that something very significant had happened in the previous week. I asked her to talk through the last week and she said that two things had happened that had left her feeling sad. One was an argument with her sibling, and the other was an incident in school where she had been told off for talking to her friends. Secretly, I was a little pleased about the talking in class incident as it was the first time she had mentioned friends, and when we discussed it further, she explained how she had spent the last couple of weeks playing with her friends more, rather than sitting on her own. We worked through her choices again and she was fully aware of the fact she made a choice that didn't leave her with the best outcome and she knew what to do next time.

We then looked at her sibling situation and spent the rest of the session focusing on all the different options available to her. The biggest barrier for Lucy to overcome was the fact that her brother's learning difficulties didn't mean she had to view the situation differently, or her outcome. She just had to look at a wider range of options. It kind of came back to the 'stop' and 'flip' of the thought process session. The negative thought about the learning difficulty could be flipped and all the positives could be looked at. As she said, her brother couldn't help how he reacted a lot of the time, and as she couldn't control his reactions and responses, it was important she focused on what she could do and how if she changed the cycle of how she responded to an incident, the way she would feel would be different, and in turn she would return to normal far more quickly. This was a real awakener for her.

Session 6 - Final Assessment

The final session bought some tears of happiness (on both parts) and also a beautiful collection of drawings to signify the work together. I had some sketches of flowers, an erupting volcano and a pair of die (I will leave you to work out your own significance to these, as I have already done it!). Lucy said that her mum had noticed a major difference and had told Lucy that she loved Jepeca and what it had done for her. She talked about how the bullying had stopped, and she wasn't really sure why but she felt so much happier in class. She even mentioned the fact that she had a boyfriend and loved playtime now as she could spend time with him and her friends. She had marked up on both her confidence and self-esteem and felt so much better. The real icing on the cake was when I asked her to describe herself and she said, "Happy, pretty and popular". This after only six hours of working together. I think I looked like a proud mother hen that day and left feeling the biggest sense of satisfaction.

One of my favourite cases.

"Elise has evolved before my eyes…"

Case Study Number 9

By Katie Dommett

Reason for referral from point of contact

Elise   12 years old   Girl   England

By the time Elise had been referred to us, every other avenue had been exhausted, literally. She had been through counselling, school support, one-to-one support inside and outside the class, and other bespoke learning and development services. The sentiment was very much that she was a 'lost cause' and there was no real expectation for any sort of turn around. It was purely another avenue that the school could go down to try and help her; a final resort, you might say. The background was harrowing, to say the least. Elise had been one of 12 children, and one of the younger ones. She had been raised initially in the family home, but was removed at five years old and subsequently placed in care until she was adopted at around 10. When she had been removed at five and assessed, it became apparent that she had no communication skills, could barely walk or eat normally, had a visible tic, and behavioural problems. Further investigation discovered a home life where the younger children had not been interacted with at all, had been left in a corner of the room and they had been witness to violence, alcoholism and abuse within the family home. There had been no level of engagement with the children to stimulate and develop their ability to talk, walk, eat properly or be toilet trained. The adoptive parents were at a loss of how to deal with the unresponsiveness of Elise and had engaged with several agencies to try and deal with this, with little success. The school were simply looking at any way to give Elise a basic foundation for when she left school, as currently she was way behind her peers and unable to communicate with the class. They wanted Elise to be able to function in the real world. Their hopes were that she would be able to find employment and live independently. Things that may seem a given for the majority of teenagers, but Elise had had such a challenging start to life that they felt at this stage, it would be a slim possibility of happening. This had to be one of the most distressing reports I had ever read.

Session 1 - Initial assessment

When I met with Elise, it did seem heartbreaking. There was hardly any eye contact and a very visible tic, which Elise was also trying to cover up by shifting in her seat a lot and moving her hands and legs, like a nervous shake to detract from the tremor. Even though I was looking at a teenage girl, it felt more like I had a five-year-old in front of me with the guarded body language and the inability to make basic conversation with me. Elise looked very grubby too. Her hair was greasy and even though her clothes looked clean, they seemed to hang off her as if she had taken no time, care or attention to dress in the morning. Her eyes seemed to be continually darting around the room but very rarely focusing on me, and at this stage, I will admit that in my mind I could hear the words of the teachers when they said, "You are the last chance, really; the final avenue to turn down".

Elise did not disclose any of her history to me in this first session. She calibrated her confidence and self-esteem as 10 and gave lots of, "Don't know," answers when I asked her about her feelings and how she felt about herself. Interestingly, when I asked her what she would like others to think of her, she replied, "Respected". I asked her what she meant by this, and she said that she wanted people to look up to her and respect her.

All of the rest of the questions I asked on the initial assessment were answered in a basic yes/no fashion, and when I asked Elise about her dreams and aspirations, she said she would like to have a job and live in her own place. This struck me as so basic, yet so taken for granted by so many people. Here was a girl who was looking for meaning in her life, and for her, that meant being able to be responsible for herself and live independently.

I felt very passionate at this stage that I could help her and told her this to ensure she had some level of confidence in me when she left the room. I explained clearly how the next few sessions would run and told her that I was here to empower her to make the changes. I wanted her to know that she would be as responsible for these changes as I would be in teaching her the techniques. Elise still seemed very guarded in her body language, but when I asked her the important question of whether she wanted to work with me over the coming weeks, she looked away and said, "Yeah".

Session 2 - Filters

The first thing that became very apparent in this next session with Elise was her inability to work in an associated manner. By this, I mean she was unable to look at her own life and use examples of things that were actually happening to her. It seemed it was too painful to actually look at ways she could filter what was being said to her, and instead, safer to look at how others can filter. When we did the bubble, we had to look at things that were happening to people she knew, or we would make up different scenarios to look at those outcomes.

I began to notice input from Elise with her coming up with different scenarios and I saw elements of her imagination coming through with the use of words that these bullies would use. The language and swear words were pretty extreme, and Elise seemed to know a wide array of swear words. For a 12-year-old girl, she seemed very confident to use severe swear words and cuss words when we carried out the bubble exercise, which gave me a little window in to the words that had been possibly used on her. It was also still clear that communicating was a real struggle with Elise, and the hunched body language and lowered eye contact showed this. I began to wonder if anyone else had ever actually spent time with Elise, focusing totally on what she wanted and not what was expected.

Elise also struggled to visualise her bubble. She found it difficult to relax and to visualise. I asked her to draw her bubble instead on the board and show me where the words would be going when they were coming towards her. We then practised this with throwing the balls to each other saying nice things, and then nasty things, with Elise either catching or letting the ball drop (depending on what she wanted to take in or not). It was a case of using a combination of different approaches to still achieve the end result, which was for Elise to recognise she had a bubble and could control what she filtered in and what she didn't. We agreed to continue the following week.

Session 3 - Thought Training and Development

When Elise came in to this week's session, she finally told me something about her weekend. Each week, we start the session by asking about something good that has happened, and then something bad. Last week, Elise had said nothing and had not disclosed anything about her previous week, but this week she talked about the fact she had been swimming over the weekend. A very small thing to mention for some, but I felt that Elise had actually communicated with me in an associated way, talking about an experience she'd had. Wonderful!

The thought training session, however, did remain in a disassociated way with other people's examples of where someone might like to go, what they might like to buy etc. The negative words were very much led by myself and Elise could not think of anything negative she might think to herself. She still seemed unable to access her own thoughts and feelings, due to how painful they were. The session was still effective and we were still able to look at how a person can make their thoughts a reality; we just hadn't really dipped in to Elise's world yet.

Session 4 - Emotional Awareness

I like to re-name 'Emotional Awareness' as my turning point session! I began the session as always, asking about good and bad things in the week and she volunteered some of her own experiences (she had watched some good TV over the weekend, but she'd had a problem at school).

We started looking at the traffic lights and what each colour meant and then moved on to the RAG itself and where you have the choices available. I asked Elise for a situation where she had experienced something that left her feeling 'amber'. This was the first session that Elise volunteered her own example and we were able to look at the choices available to her. She explained how a group of girls and boys had been bullying her, in particular, at lunchtime and how they had been saying nasty things about her tic and the way she looked. She was very angry and we devoted nearly the whole hour on this particular scenario. The reason we focused on the one situation was because Elise felt that the only choices available to her were violent choices. I believed that this was a really good thing to work on, as I was seeing Elise truly experience this feeling of anger and really not knowing what to do with it. We were working associated and in the moment, and as she started to say that she wanted to beat them up, follow them home from school, swear at them and lots of other violent options, I saw her communicating with me finally. I felt it was needed for her to get this pent-up aggression and anger out, and to see how it would eventually impact her so she saw that the person then responsible for how she would be left feeling would be her. We had a lot of reality bubbles on the whiteboard in red, flowing further and further down the whiteboard as the negative choices left Elise feeling worse and worse. It felt slightly cathartic, and whilst I knew we still had a lot of work to do, I actually began to see a personality and a change in expression and tone from Elise that I hadn't experienced prior to this. Elise was eventually able to look at some different choices that may give her a better outcome, and one involved taking up a lunchtime club on creative writing. She said that she liked writing but wasn't very good at it, and when we looked at this option, it became a green bubble, a positive reality for her that would mean something else to focus on and also taking her out of the situation with the bullies and feeling vulnerable to them.

Towards the end of the session, Elise started to talk a little more about one particular bully and mentioned that this bully knew she was adopted. She asked me if I had known and I said that I did. She began to talk about her biological family and whilst she didn't go in to masses of detail, she confirmed for me that she had witnessed violence, that she knew her parents were alcoholics and that it hadn't been a great environment for her to grow up in. It was amazing to see her actually communicate but then I was again left wondering if she had ever been allowed this opportunity before. I knew she'd had counselling and maybe she had disclosed there, but with me she seemed to want to start looking at what had happened and how she felt about it and what she could do about it. In my mind, very productive, and for someone who was deemed a "lost cause", quite outstanding.

Session 5 - Communication

Our session on communication was inspiring, and really for the simple fact that I actually saw Elise communicate with me. She wrote on the board and spoke as she wrote, which had been near on impossible in the first couple of weeks due to her tic. I had noticed as the weeks had passed that the tic had become less noticeable. I asked Elise if she felt the same and she said this was the first time she had ever written on the board and she wanted to try it in class too. We were also now starting all our sessions with an update on what happened in their previous week. This was normal practise with all my children but had been particularly difficult with Elise in the beginning, as she had struggled with verbalising anything. I was now hearing more about what she was doing and also about her home life and a sister she lived with (a biological sister that the family had also adopted). She seemed noticeably happier and asked if she could work with me again as she felt she wanted to go back through everything she had learnt. In this instance, I felt it would be really beneficial, as Elise had started to work in an associated manner so the request was put forward and we did complete the programme again.

Session 6 - Final Assessment

Our final session confirmed to me that we should never give up on a person, and if they want the help, then there is always hope. Elise had evolved before my eyes in to a girl who was able to make eye contact, was able to talk about her own feelings in as much as ,"I feel happy / sad / angry / confused etc." She was someone who had become more vocal in class and who was actually getting involved in debates in class. Her tic had calmed down massively, and she was also aware of this, and above everything, she told me she felt happier. She looked better too, as if she had begun to take a little more pride in her appearance. Her hair was cleaner and her clothes looked as if they had been put on, rather than slung on.

She felt that her ambition to get a job and to live independently was realistic and she knew the steps she had to take to get there. She said she felt less angry at the world, and although she still didn't like school massively, she knew that for her to achieve what she wanted, she had to complete school. Things seemed genuinely better and she had started the creative writing class, which she was enjoying. When we completed the programme again the following term, the focus became very much on how Elise coped with her change in feelings and the anger and frustration she felt about her childhood. We used the Jepeca Cycle several times throughout this, as it was important for Elise to see that, by continuing to respond and behave in the same way, she was achieving the same result. We worked on changing the response and Elise using her new techniques of the bubble, her new interests and actually communicating with people to let them know how she was feeling. By doing this, she was in a far better state and witnessing a very different reaction. We also looked at what she could control and also recognising that what happened in her childhood was the best that her biological parents could offer at that time. Elise had no control over this but did have control of her present and future and the choice she would now make.

Elise really inspired me because it showed me that even in real adversity and when all others have lost hope around you, inner strength and confidence and a drive to succeed will always shine through, and with Elise, I know that she will succeed in her life because she really wants too. I feel proud that I have reignited in her that inner strength and showed her that she had it there the whole time; she just needed to know how to use it.

"We are delighted with the outcome
of the Jepeca programme;
it was very positive."

Commissioning Jepeca

Teachers

If you are a head teacher, teacher or SENCO, and would like to commission Jepeca to empower your young people, then contact us at resources@jepeca.com

Our coaches have enhanced DBS checks, CP, Insured, first aid training, and offer a professional, reliable service providing a detailed report for each client. We work with Year 5 (age 9 to 10 years) upwards.

The positive impact Jepeca has on schools is reflected in their budgets, time, resources and results.

Parents

We DO NOT work with young people in their homes.

If you are concerned or worried about your son or daughter's emotional health and well-being, then contact us at info@jepeca. com

We will discuss your options and how we can make a difference, or you can contact your school, college or university and ask them to contact us.

GPs or Social Services

Fast, effective and measurable, achieving 92% positive change. Contact resources@jepeca.com for more information and to discuss how we can make a difference in your environment.

"It's like teaching a different child."

Jepeca's Vision

Jepeca is continually growing and evolving, and because there will always be challenges and changes throughout life, we understand the importance of understanding and enhancing your natural abilities to make informed decisions and live a happy, in control and productive life.

There are so many unhappy, sad, lonely, desperate, scared, angry, annoyed, frustrated, confused, worried, stressed young people with no idea how to make the changes that they want to see in their world, and that is why Jepeca coaches strive to provide what we know to be a successful programme that will make a significant difference and change lives.

We are very successful at what we do, and in order to maintain this standard of quality, we operate a very structured and regulated service across the board.

My vision is to have the Jepeca programme accessible to every young person so that our next generation will be happy, in control and productive. Any and all help in this mission is greatly appreciated. Together, we can, and will, empower the world – one young person at a time.

6327847R00106

Printed in Great Britain
by Amazon.co.uk, Ltd.,
Marston Gate.